Translated from the French by WILLIAM SAYERS

Foreword by JULIA KRISTEVA

CORNELL UNIVERSITY PRESS *Ithaca*

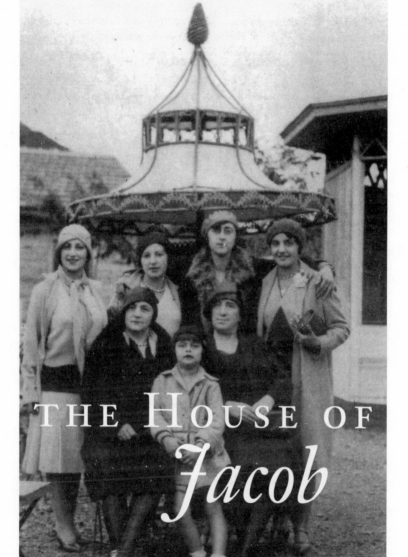

THE HOUSE OF
Jacob

SYLVIE COURTINE-DENAMY

La Maison de Jacob: La langue pour seule patrie, by Sylvie Courtine-Denamy (copyright Editions Phébus, 2001), is the winner of the 2002 Alberto Benveniste Prize for Literature.

This translation was prepared with the generous assistance of the French Ministry of Culture–Centre National du Livre (ouvrage publié avec le concours du Ministère français chargé de la culture Centre National du Livre).

First published 2003 by Cornell University Press

Printed in the United States of America

Library of Congress Cataloging-in-Publication Data

Courtine-Denamy, Sylvie.
  [Maison de Jacob. English]
  The house of Jacob / Sylvie Courtine-Denamy ; translated from the French by William Sayers ; foreword by Julia Kristeva.
    p. cm.
  ISBN 0-8014-4065-3 (cloth : alk. paper)
  1. Cuenca family. 2. Gabay family. 3. Jews—France—Biography. 4. Sephardim—France—Biography. 5. Holocaust survivors—France—Biography. 6. Jews—France—Genealogy. I. Title.
  DS135.F89C6813 2003
  929'.2'08992404—dc21
                                        2003005596

Cloth printing   10 9 8 7 6 5 4 3 2 1

Para Yacob i Esterika

All troubles can be borne
if you make a story of them
and if you tell them.
                                        —Isak Dinesen

Contents

Foreword:
    Languages as One's Only Homeland,
    by Julia Kristeva ix
Acknowledgments xvii

I IN THE LAND OF SEPHARAD 1
    1. "Zakhor!" 3
    2. Cuenca, the Memory of Origins 9

II INTO THE LANDS OF THE GRAND TURK 27
    1. Varna: "Cuenca Brothers" 35
    2. Salonika 42

       Moïse and Allegra 42
       Mathilde and Marguerite 47
    3. Constantinople 50
       On the European Shore, in the Galatasaray
          Quarter 50
       On the Asiatic Shore 59

III BETWEEN EAST AND WEST: A TIME FOR ALLIANCES 71
    1. The Cuenca Michpaha 75
    2. The Gabay Michpaha 88

IV DRANCY 97
    1. The Return 99
    2. From the Partisans to the Camps of Upper Silesia:
       Robert 106
    3. Bayonne and Its Jews: Marie and Fortunée 114

V IN FRENCH TERRITORIAL WATERS 123
    1. A Wedding Night at the Péra Palas 125
    2. In the House of Jacob 130

    Notes 147
    Glossary 153
    References 161
    Index 165

Foreword: Languages as One's Only Homeland

My dear Sylvie,

I received the manuscript for your latest book like a fresh spring shower. This impression may seem paradoxical to you, for your text is full of suffering, crisscrossed as it is by the long memory of exile, from the city of Cuenca in Spain—where your paternal family originated and knew pogroms from 1388 onward—until today. It is woven of the memories of trials, echoes of the Inquisition and death camps, the specters of hospitals and illnesses, and dramas of every kind. When you told me about it, over lunch in Jussieu or Montparnasse, your grief carried me along in its wake and my mood darkened to the point of losing the thread of what the philosopher in me had to say about Hannah Arendt or your *Three Women in Dark Times*. But in your account I found both the distance of history and the proximity of dialogue with those closest to you, and this calmed, even reinvigorated, me.

As a historian, you taught me details about the Sephardic community of which I was ignorant, a community which I had, however, known well in my native Bulgaria, about the persecutions it suffered, and its extraordinary perseverance. Extraordinary is perhaps not the word, for, on the contrary—and your whole book bears the mark—this Jewish people whose itinerary you recreate, who fled the Inquisition, who crossed Europe to the Balkans, traveled the length and breadth of Turkey before returning, as your parents did, to France, is infused with a simplicity that can tame the ordinary, precisely so as to rejoice in it and pass it on. You remain open to that gift of everyday simplicity in your effort to remember: *Zakhor!*

That memory that you sought among the historians and in the archives is animated by your use of the familiar pronoun *tu* when addressing your forebears, right down, quite naturally, to Abba and Ima. The monologue that you direct to them collapses time into a single indefinite moment, and this familiarity of the instant makes me, the reader, a contemporary of a long lineage that, through the artifice of your use of *tu*, transforms your ancestors into my contemporaries. A certain life, the life of your love for them, becomes contagious. And, without forgetting their tragedy, I draw from your family a vitality through their continuation in you, a spirit incarnated in the familiar *tu* you use when writing of a great-grandfather or an aunt who has disappeared in the Holocaust or somewhere between Varna, Salonika, and Constantinople.

It is then that the torrent of your text, which surprises and troubles me, is transformed into a refreshing rain, into an intimacy that reinvigorates. And I will not forget the perfumes of the Orient that saturate your history, to the point of imposing themselves like the true doublet of that Judeo-Spanish or Ladino that you cherish. And I ask myself whether it is true that your people had only a single homeland, their language, and whether it is only thanks to that language that they have survived, or, rather, thanks to the taste of dishes and scents that haunt them, that haunt you.

Ah! the house of Jacob, its words, its foods, its melodies! I, too, have known them, in a different way, since my maternal grandmother's name was Jecov, in the Slavic manner, and I hear her still: "Ande ir en galut? En las tyerras del Grande Turko"; "Aman, aman, aman!"; "imam baïldi"; "Kukla mia, kokona," without mentioning Sabbatai Zevi, and that's not the end of it. But, in the religious and ethnic intermingling of the Balkans—and taking into account the tolerance if not friendship (let's not fantasize!) that Bulgarians showed toward the Jews, and which you very accurately portray—my family was Christian. And for my part, rightly or wrongly, after an education in the spirit of the Enlightenment, I no longer sense in myself any identity capable of being categorized in terms of religious, ethnic, or national affiliation. Like the dark ironist that was Proust, I try not to "be one of them," it's difficult enough just to *be*. But this is another story, and now is not the time to address it. I mention it to you, as you know, only in terms of taste, when we happen to eat *kefte*, *filas*, or *malebis* together.

Your mother's illness, Esther's *dibuk*, as you call it, and her death, which discreetly but irremediably rips through the final pages of your text, seems to me to be the intimate source of your writing. I imagine, but this is perhaps only a projection, that this mourning gave you the energy you needed to fulfill the testament, the *zakhor!* of Jacob, your father. But here, too, I have nothing to tell you, and it remains for you to continue to write this feminine passion, this enigmatic tie of daughter and mother, while continuing to meditate, as you have already done, on the epic of great Jewish women who have succeeded in transforming their *dibuks* into radiant accomplishments.[1]

There is an idea in your book that gives me pause, more so than these themes that so overwhelm me when reading your text—a central idea, it seems to me, that you see as the root of this Sephardic diaspora, but one that might well find echoes beyond this specific community: "language as one's only homeland."

Whether they are called Cuenca, Coenca, Kohenka, or Denamy (to speak only of the patronymics of the Cuenca *michpaha*, without mentioning those of the Gabay *michpaha*), whether they pass through Istanbul, Biarritz, Bordeaux, or Varna, these exiled ancestors nonetheless have a homeland: their language, Judeo-Spanish, which originated in the Castilian of the fourteenth and fifteenth centuries and which absorbed influences from the languages with which the migratory Jewish populations came into contact (Greek, Turkish, Arabic, French). You delight in recalling this and even have a glossary at the end of your book. Here we have an archaic language that, however, developed in the company of others.[2] It preserves the memory of Spain before the Inquisition, the Spain of Alfonso VIII, for example, who in 1190 granted Jews the same rights as Christians. Although the accommodation of Jews and Christians found in Spain in those distant times may have been less idyllic than some have claimed (and you present incontrovertible proof of this), it would seem that the "flight from Spain" preserved, in the shadows of memory, a "Golden Age," an age of well-being that was crystallized and preserved in the jealous safeguarding of this old Spanish language, the land of which, however, had been lost.

Judeo-Spanish, close to the language of the inquisitors—we know that an executioner can be the object of fascination—admittedly remained above all the language of domestic happiness, of the reassuring hearth, all honey and spices. The glossary that you give us offers the proof: it is full of terms for foods and the senses, the profane lexicon of daily feelings, of tenderness or anger, of recognition, ties, rituals, kinship. Ethnicity in its maternal, sensory, instinctive, passionate valences is expressed here—as a counterpart of that religious exaltation for the Law of the Father, perhaps somewhat out of step with that Law but certainly in harmony with it and, why not, as a respite from its sacral exaltation, even forgetting it for a moment. Is Judeo-Spanish the language of sensory time, in counterpoint to that language conceived and practiced as a symbolic code, as is the case with the Law and the Forbidden? "After all, it is not the German language that went mad!" exclaimed Hannah Arendt after Auschwitz, thus rejecting a question that to all appearances did more than just torment her.[3] An inapplicable statement with respect to Judeo-Spanish, because it goes back to an older Castilian, far distant from modern Francoisms; and perhaps especially because its sensuality, preserved in the mouths and bonds of family, kept it apart from the history that raged around it.

Entirely different is Yiddish. Under the sway of German and in proximity with the Slavic languages, in the aura of the Romantic movement that consecrated the cult of language as a modern divinity and consequently as the "seat of being," Yiddish was able to create an exceptional oral but also written literature, which boasts the best modern writers of Jewish origin, from Franz Kafka to Philip Roth. Judeo-Spanish, that "only homeland," as you call it, seems on the contrary to withdraw—modestly? proudly?—into the world of senses and the universe of kinship. A fascinating folklore and a dedicated publishing enterprise continue to perpetuate its values, but you fear that its savor may be lost, that with this language, which is a taste, may disappear not only the memory of your kin but also one of the destinies of Judaism: its European diaspora that survived the horrors of antisemitism to nourish itself on a certain pleasure in life, characteristic, when we come down to it, of the peoples of the south, the peoples of southern Europe in particular.

I understood better, I think, between the lines of your account, the "mad" ambition of Eliezer Ben-Yehuda to impose Hebrew on Israel, as well as the anguish of Gershom Scholem at this prospect. Ben-Yehuda, you'll remember, in his book *Le Rêve traversé* tells us how, twenty years before Herzl exposed the "Jewish problem," he himself decided to settle in Jerusalem with the resurrection of Hebrew as his sole objective.[4] At the risk of sacrificing wife and children to that noble but debatable cause and at once attracting the anger of the orthodox, he succeeded in imposing the language of the holy texts as the current language, the secular language of everyday, one that you had a right to use even with your dog! By thus defundamentalizing Hebrew, by making it into a national language, Ben-Yehuda created the fact of a Jewish nation, more so perhaps even than the political Zionists did. As Gérard Haddad writes, echoing Lacan, Ben-Yehuda made Hebrew into the paternal metaphor that the citizens of Israel lacked. He embedded in each person the symbol of Yahweh, since Hebrew, in the daily life of that country, gave expression to the Name-of-the-Father that the Bible celebrates. Although it is still true that none of the problems of the Jewish state have been resolved at the present time, because of the prolonged Middle Eastern crisis, Hebrew, contrary to Herzl's fears, now represents the solution to the language problem, since it is definitively the language of the Jews of Israel as well as that of an increasing number of those of the diaspora.

We should not, however, underestimate Scholem's concern, formulated, it is true, in 1926, in a blurred and distant past: he questions this "actualization" of the Hebrew language, "pregnant with catastrophe," he fears, because it is composed of "religious terms employed without discernment," "rudimentary, almost ghostly," "without tradition." Scholem thinks of the tradition of the "spoken," of that of the "Voice," which he hopes to "hear again," and for this he counts on the forces of a "youth capable of confronting the revolt of a sacred language." He fears that a "crude imitation" of the sacred language by a purely utilitarian language will destroy the symbolic sense that makes up the unconscious basis of language and of culture itself, expressed through it. I like to imagine as well that Scholem wanted to infuse a Hebrew that had become increasingly utilitarian—even while initially remaining too bookish and sacral—with the liveliness of the "spoken," such as one hears in the German poetry on which Scholem himself was nourished, or in Yiddish or Judeo-Spanish. And he prophesied that if this repressed "tradition" reawakened someday, it would take the form of an uncontrollable explosion of religious forces.[5]

Hebrew has then unquestionably imposed itself as a language of modern culture as well as of religious culture, despite the fears of this great thinker, although his warnings have not lost their importance. But it is the real development of Israeli democracy, with all its conflicts and the contributions of various communities of immigrants, bearers of their own linguistic and cultural traditions, that may one day harmonize the mixture—an explosive one—of the sacred and the profane that Hebrew entails, and which so impressed Scholem.

The destiny of the Judeo-Spanish language is quite another matter. Marginalized, even threatened with oblivion—an oblivion that risks sweeping away the very history of all those who have spoken it, and against which you, Sylvie, have risen up, instilled with the memorialist's sense of duty your father bequeathed to you. It is crucial not to forget what Europe has experienced, how it has constituted itself as it is today, and what it has imposed on those who were an integral part of its culture, economy, riches, progress, sensations, tastes, languages.

We can thus make out another face of Jewishness in your account, one that does not occupy the forefront of current politics but which is no less rewarding. You call attention to the Judaism of the diaspora, in particular the Sephardic experience, which has opted in favor of a dichotomy: Hebrew, the sacred language, on the one hand; Judeo-Spanish, the language of the senses, on the other. In the absence of any great literary accomplishment in the latter— Elias Canetti, born in Bulgaria of Judeo-Spanish parents, is a British author writing in German—the ideals of the French Enlightenment have served as the "paternal signifier," as the "symbolic law" for many of those who belonged to the land of *djudyo*. New sciences and technologies, cutting-edge research, the esthetic avant-garde, psychoanalysis, and even the revolutionary ideologies of the twentieth century have caught their attention. But the Sephardim prefer to express their emotions in proverbs, tales, *romansas*. Less directly confronted with Nazism, whose full force was borne by the Ashkenazim, the Sephardim fell victim to the more insidious southern variants of totalitarianism. And lay culture exerted a no less liberating charm. France: land of exile; the French language: haven for Judeo-Spanish; "human rights": in exchange for the Bible? How many hopes and how many cruel disappointments, with Vichy and Drancy at their terminus—your *abba* knew what he was talking about: "Zakhor!"

When all that will have been said, when "repentance" and the "duty of memory" cease to be pious wishes and become real for us— oh, I know, little by little and with all the possible and imaginable limits that implies!—then perhaps from a fresh perspective we could rethink the Sephardic diaspora that had "language as one's only homeland." Neither soil, nor blood, nor faith. Could that Europe, which we are attempting to construct with such difficulty, be its horizon, and its languages, in the plural, be our only homeland?

I say "our" because in the European citizenship that is taking shape, so long as we are not globalized by Anglo-American culture, are we not all persons with one native language (say, French) who then migrated into other languages (English, Spanish, Italian, German, Russian, Swedish)? It is no longer the Inquisition or Nazism that drives us from home and hearth but the needs of technology that force us to cross borders, or even make us come to love this nomadism. We believe, for the first time in history, that humanity is not defined by its habitat, or is so defined only to a limited extent. Haven't the Jews of the diaspora already shown the way? Like them, we nevertheless preserve a language of sensation, the maternal, gustatory code of our childhood palate, and then graft onto it elements picked up here and there during our journeys.

What then will be the "paternal signifier" of this new wandering? Whose task will it be to stabilize it, to give it meaning—or finally, and preferably, open it to continuous interrogation? Hebrew? The code of science? Psychoanalysis? The philosophy of human rights? The question remains open . . . and opens onto the abyss.

But it would seem that a polyphonic humanity is already in the making, and that it does not have a single language. It will be more expatriate than your ancestors, at home in their Ladino and Judeo-Spanish, for better or, often, for worse. Nothing prevents us from hoping, however, that this may also be for the best. For the language I speak determines the way I feel and the way I interrogate the world. And if it is true that my exile is my tragedy, it is also a blessing, since it sharpens and multiplies my perceptions and my questions. It remains for me to convince those around me, who do not yet share this destiny, to risk this wandering, to hear the polyphonies for themselves. We would then once and for all have created Europe, the Europe that has not forgotten that it took in, expelled, killed, and fascinated the Cuencas and Gabays, but that also remembers them, paying homage to the complexity of their experience and profiting from the hope that they placed in it. This is the hard part, and it remains to be done. Thank you, my dear Sylvie, for having raised these questions in a way that you alone could do.

JULIA KRISTEVA

Acknowledgments

The French edition of this book was supported by a Mission Stendhal grant. Thanks are due to Yves Mabin for the fine trip to the Land of Sepharad.

The author also wishes to thank the Center for Contemporary Jewish Documentation, the French National Archives, and the diocesan archives of the city of Cuenca, which made this work possible.

Lastly, her gratitude goes to all members of this large family, scattered throughout the world, who have been kind enough to share their memories with her: Allegra Yeroham-Akşiyote (Mexico City), Jo Cuenca (Cali), Beky Kohen-Roza (Jerusalem), Klara Gabay-

Maillard (Paris), Sultana Gabay-Barzilay (Paris), the late Flora Salti-Behar (Fort Lauderdale), Robert Frances (Paris), Rita Vradjali-Fisher (New York), Tico Vradjali-Barzilay (Haifa), Rita Houlon-Jaulus (San Francisco), Gloria Behar-Gottsegen (Boca Raton), Vivianne Cuenca-Azcarate (Houston), Buby Frances (Paris), Jacques Policar (Paris), Hemo and Jacquita Pappo (Paris), Moïse and Rita Kohen (Paris), Claude Saporta (Marseille), the late Hélène Kaufman-Cuenca (Paris), Solly Benador-Hatem (Istanbul), and to the first among them all who prompted her to find them, Rita Frances-Bacon (Saint Cloud).

THE HOUSE OF *Jacob*

I

IN THE LAND OF SEPHARAD

*. . . de donde fuymos echados,
y en malo modo*

Spain . . . from which we were expelled,
and in very foul fashion
                    —E. Morin, *Vidal et les siens*

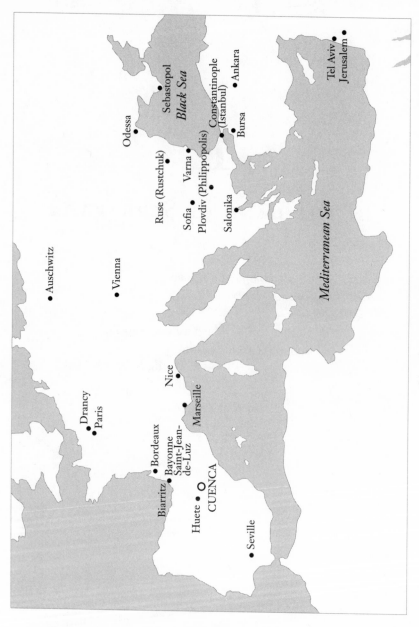

Map of the Sephardic Diaspora

I

"Zakhor!"

I could not succeed in erasing from my memory the last image of my parents lying in their coffins. Both had died in the hospital. *Ima*, who was sick, had refused to accompany her own husband to his last resting place, leaving me to face alone the terrible event of burying a father. Early that morning, I had gone to the Pontoise morgue. I had not kissed my father for a last time, still heeding the advice to "avoid all close contact." The custodian asked me, "Do you wish to see him?" I had moved closer. They raised the lid. I recognized *Abba*, rigid, hairs sticking out of his nose, his nails too long, in his smart brown-striped suit from Chez Charles, his Greek tailor on the Champs-Élysées. They prevented me from sitting beside the coffin in the hearse that took us to the cemetery in Pantin, so that I had to get in next to the driver, who tried to take my mind off things when we got caught in traffic. I was afraid of being late. A few years later, I would approach the body of my dead mother in the same fashion. A white angora cap pulled down over her skull, her hands tightly clasped in a last spasm—who had dressed the bluish body of Ima for the last time?

> *La vida es un pasaje*
> *Por ganar avantaje.*
> *La muerte es un viaje*
> *Al mundo de la verdad.*

> Life is a passage
> From which one hopes to profit.
> Death is a voyage
> To the land of truth.[1]

So Jacob was the first to leave me. In the beginning I didn't want to believe it, but however much I cried—as loudly as Shifrah Leah when Alter, her husband, died—I could not succeed as she had in re-calling him to the world of the living.[2] All those tender words that I would never hear again, that warm look when I appeared, that need to touch me, those crazy kisses, a *modrisko.*

Jacob and I had the same looks. When I was little, people used to laugh when they saw us together, such look-alikes, "the spitting image of her father." Jacob said he was flattered, I was proud, Ima was piqued: "She doesn't take after me at all." "She's a Cuenca," added Jacob, "the image of Régine." Régine, your beloved sister, *Rejinika de bonbon*, the sweet, lively aunt from America, whose suitcases were stuffed with records, with autographs of Paul Anka. For me, Jacob, you were exotic: your improbable accent when you made an effort to roll your r's in order to seem "more French"! When I was little, I admired your confidence, your know-how: everywhere we went, you knew how to get served promptly. For me your recollec-tions were spellbinding, the names you spoke magical: Istanbul, Ankara, Prenkipo, Büyük Ada, Bursa, Philippolis, Varna, Sofia, Galata, Vienna, Leipzig, Hamburg, Hinterzarten . . . That song we taped together—this was before television—with Eddie Constantine and his daughter: "Tell me, handsome sir, is the earth really round?" . . . Your way of going into a bar, of picking up the mike: "Besame, besame mucho," "Qué buenitos ojos tienes," "Strangers in the Night." The songs the three of us used to sing on our trips. We would never go again and sit with cousin Salomon on the red imitation leather benches at the restaurant Les Diamantaires, feasting on *imam baïldi*.

> *Se fue mi viejo, el mundo me lo yevo*
> *I agora el viejo soy yo.*
>
> My old man is gone, the world took him from me
> And now it's me who is the old one.

Since the death of my parents, since I became an orphan, I have assumed the duty of memory. "Zakhor,"[*] Jacob had always counseled me: "Remember"—but without explaining what or why! I was aware that I had picked up only inadequate bits and pieces of my family's history. I had waited for the two of you to die to haunt the places of your childhood, to appropriate your memories. It is true, Abba, that you had always refused to take me to Turkey, your native country, because you were so bitter over your deportation to the camp of Aşkale in Anatolia, where for two years running you were put to work building roads. This, in fact, was the fate reserved for those who had not been able to pay within fifteen days the *varlik vergisi*, a tax on capital, decreed on 16 November 1942 and implemented in January 1943, which taxed Jews at the rate of 179 percent of their annual income![3]

Never forget . . . but forget what? That you are Jewish. Always come forward, reveal yourself. Very early in my life, instead of the cross and the medal of the Virgin Mary that hung around others' necks, I wanted the *mezuza*, the little cylinder enclosing the tablets of

---

[*] Judeo-Spanish words and loans from other languages are explained in a glossary at the end of the book.

the Law, my Jewishness. Yet, I suffered like a martyr when "Napoleon"—a nickname given to the thunder-voiced head proctor on the third floor of my fine, airy high school, always smelling of fresh floor wax—bellowed into the classroom, "Anna, Sara . . . the rabbi is waiting for you!" and we had to comply under the mocking eyes of our classmates, who would take their solemn first communion in those beautiful white dresses that we would never wear. From the Hebrew classes I remembered only the colored pictures in a little book that, strangely, was read from right to left, only a single phrase, *ima baa*, "mama is coming." Of the rabbi, only the memory of an insignificant little man who, nevertheless, sent me out of the classroom when I insolently taunted him: "At our place we eat ham sandwiches!"

Zakhor, never forget . . . but what then? The "Shema Israël" that my father and sometimes my mother gravely recited when they took a plane, bringing the mezuza to their lips? The joy-filled details of festivities that followed the holy day of Yom Kippur, which Ima had begun to observe after the death of her father? For a long time, as a little girl, I felt humiliated when it was my turn to kiss the thin, emaciated hand of the patriarch—Merkado, my grandpa—who in return blessed me in a language that I had refused to hear, a language that ever afterward I would miss.

Zakhor, never forget! But just what? Of Jewish ritual I had made no effort to preserve anything more than gastronomical memories, the few family ceremonies that took us to the temple on the rue de la Victoire or, more commonly, to the ENIO, the Eastern Jewish Teacher Training College, which my Gabay grandparents used to go to.

Remember, but what? Did the family have some hero, some resistance fighter to be proud of? Did we have some martyr to mourn? Did Ima, a student at the Molière high school, have to put on her school uniform one fine morning, a yellow star sewn on the lapel, and on her face the shame of a girl who was "not like the others"? Remember . . .

Yet, in my own way, I had absorbed Abba's injunction. At the age of ten, when I was in my first year at middle school, I was brutally confronted with its meaning when Dédé, a little girl with long black braids, had shouted in the face of another girl who would become my friend—although I didn't know it at the time—the despicable words "dirty little Jew!" Silent, Anna went pale. Then I grabbed Dédé's pigtails, pulled hard, and shouted very loudly. I didn't say a word about this incident at home. But Anna had told her parents. Anna's father wanted to meet the brave little Jewess. And so a friendship was born.

Zakhor: "We were a big family; today we're spread all over," wrote Beky, one of Ima's cousins who had emigrated to Jerusalem and was the custodian of the Avigdor family memory, when I was struggling to put together the puzzle of the family tree. For my part, I had been "conceived in French territorial waters" and was born in the very exclusive American Hospital in Neuilly, France. However, my parents changed their name, in order to protect me, they assured me, from a new flood of grief. Abba had told me that *Coenca*, which had become *Kohenka* through the vagaries of turkization, in fact went back to the Castilian city of Cuenca, where our family had been residents before their expulsion from Spain. He had not given me the key to "our" house in Spain—was it because I was not the son Francis they had been waiting for? Or had he misplaced it himself? Had it perhaps not even been handed down to him? Was this tradition unknown to him?

I nevertheless decided to undertake the journey to the Castile of my ancestors. My friend Luisito, a painter, introduced me in turn to one of his friends, Fernando, then the mayor of Cuenca, who had created one of the most beautiful museums of modern art in Spain.

"Como te llamas?" Fernando asked me.

"Me llamo Cuenca."

Fernando seemed very moved and quickly left, assuring me that he would be right back.

Languid with the heat, gazing from the Mangana Tower out over the meandering Huecar River that curled around the foot of the modern city of Cuenca, I found Bernard Lazare's "The Cosmopolitan's Letter" coming to mind.

Where is our homeland?

"Where we have suffered?"

Then it is everywhere. It is in Rome, it is in the dark towns of Germany and Bohemia.

"Where we have loved?"

Then it is in Spain, it is in Poland.

"Our Homeland, made up of so many things, so many memories, regrets, joys, tears, sorrows that a little plot of desolate wasteland could never support it and Jerusalem, like Judea, is only one of the lots of which our homeland is made."[4]

I had read *Emek ha-bakha*[5] by my fellow countryman Joseph Hacohen, and, just as he had predicted, I found my eyes were streaming. The history of the Jews, was it not one great vale of tears? In conscientious fashion I had prepared for my trip. I knew that Jews claimed to take their name from the tribe of Judah, superior in descent to all the other sons of Jacob—with this claim authorized by the blessing of the dying patriarch himself. I knew as well that their presence in Spain was attested from the time of the Visigoths and that traces of them had been found in Castile from as early as the second half of the tenth century. *Avia sekolos ke la Espanya era su patria*: was it possible that their fate would have been a kinder one in Spain?

The year 1391 saw pogroms in Seville; 1492, the decree of expulsion. Had Bernard Lazare possibly chosen to preserve only a portion of the history of the Jews of Spain?

2

Cuenca, the Memory of Origins

I had reached that point in my reflections when my new friend Fernando returned, out of breath. Kneeling half seriously, half comically before me, offering me on a makeshift cushion a huge key of rusted iron, and still greatly moved, he named me in a single breath: *Mi reinya*, my queen! Here he was giving me much more than the key to the ancestral house; he was giving me the key to "my" city, and, guided by its mayor, I undertook the climb through the steep streets of Cuenca, pretending to believe that its old women, all dressed in black, were bowing as I passed.

Who better than its mayor could tell me the history of Cuenca? The question of the name, in particular, intrigued me: Cuenca certainly didn't sound "Jewish." And, in fact, I learned that according to the ancient cosmographers, Cuenca, founded on the borders of the kingdom of the Celts, had successively been given several different names.

"Perched like an eagle's nest on its prominent rock, to which the *casas colgadas*, the 'hanging houses' for which it is famous, would later cling, Cuenca was first called Anitorgis. But, once this town had been destroyed, the Romans constructed on its ruins the foundations of a new town, which they named Valera, 'the high place.' "

"As opposed to the 'lower town,' the modern city that we just went through?" I interjected.

"That's right," my informant replied. "And this hypothesis is also confirmed by the cosmographers when they designated the population of the period with the term *populi valeriani*. On the other hand, for Pliny, Quintilian, Strabo, and Titus-Livy, Cuenca was called Sucro, after the name of the river that runs past it, today called the Huecar. In antiquity, as you know, cities and towns were commonly named after major rivers. But other writers give the town an even more ancient origin, attributing its founding, like that of Urgel and Tarancon, to Hercules."

Admiring the marvelous, oblong, shining shell of light that limned the town, I preferred, for my part, the hypothesis according to which *Cuenca* would be a deformation of Latin *Cocaua* which means the same as *concha* or conch shell. I was equally attracted to the idea that its population was descended from the Massagetes of Scythia, who were also called Lesbians, a people so cruel that they mixed milk with horse dung to strengthen and toughen themselves for battle, to the point that they were identified with the inhabitants of Numantia.[1]

Fernando then went on about the history of the Jews in Cuenca. The town had fallen into the hands of the Arabs around 711, just after the conquest of Toledo by Tarik ben Zeyak. Three centuries later, Ismail beni Dilnun, the lord of Ucles, took control and made Cuenca the capital of the province. It had scarcely come under the rule of the Castilian king Alfonso VI, who took Toledo in 1085, when it fell into Muslim hands again, more exactly, to Almetabamid ben Abbad, king of Seville. In any case, by the end of the *Reconquista*, the town was definitively returned to Alfonso VIII (1158–1214) on 21 September 1177. The king established his residence in what became his favorite town, where his son Prince Fernando was born. Cuenca then had only eight hundred inhabitants, and so he undertook to repopulate it, creating a new bishopric and converting the mosque into a cathedral. The *judería*, the Jewish quarter established in the neighborhood of the fortress, was substantial, as its tax contribution to the royal exchequer indicates. In 1190, Alfonso VIII undertook to give Cuenca a *fuero*, or charter, that conferred on Jews the same rights as Christians by allowing them to settle freely and engage in commercial activity without restrictions. But the decrees of the Fourth Lateran Council at the beginning of the reign of Fernando III (1217–52) imposed a tithe on their lands, the wearing of special clothes, even insignia. His successor, Alfonso X (1252–84), required of Jews great simplicity in their dress and jewelry, and he undertook to prevent Christians from having dealings with them for fear of their proselytizing. He forbade Christians to consume the food and wine that Jews sent them, and he restricted Jews' civil rights, as he did those of Muslims and heretics. Alfonso was the author of the celebrated law code *Las Siete Partidas*, which, however, did not come into force until the fourteenth century. It recommended that Jews be allowed to live among Christians in the capacity of witnesses to the Crucifixion and proscribed the use of force to convert them, in favor of persuasion through examples and the words of Holy Scripture.[2] This same king, called *el Sabio*, the Wise, who claimed respect for all three religions, for the Sabbath and Jewish holy days, and who surrounded himself with Jewish counselors, nevertheless arrested and hanged Don Isaac ibn Zadok, or Don Çag de la Maleha in Castilian, the son of the most powerful Jew at his court, when in 1278 he failed in his mission to collect money for the army and navy stationed at Algeciras. Prince Sancho had in fact appropriated this sum and had spent it for his own purposes. Even if synagogues were sacred in his eyes, the faithless king did not hesitate, one Sabbath day in January 1281, to decree the arrest of all the Jews in their synagogues, not releasing them until they had paid 4,380,000 gold maravedis.

"What explains such a change of attitude?" I ventured.

"Quite simply the concentration of money in the hands of fifty to one hundred Jewish families at the end of the thirteenth century. They were paying annual taxes amounting to 70,872 maravedis and had thus aroused the hatred and envy of Christians! And so, in May 1285, the new ruler, Sancho el Bravo, lent his support to a petition by the town, which demanded judicial reform to limit the interest rate on loans made by Jews and demanded as well that no Christian be imprisoned for debt. In May 1293 he had to give in to the Cortes, the parliament, which demanded the exclusion of Jews from the office of tax collector and the abrogation of the special privileges favoring their activity as moneylenders, and which also forbade them from acquiring real estate. From 1313 onward the Council of Zamora sought to force Jews to wear distinctive insignia, to forbid them from circulating freely from Wednesday to Saturday and during all of Holy Week, and, finally, to prevent them from working on Sundays. In addition, the appointment of Samuel Halevi to the office of royal treasurer in 1353, a renewal of the tradition of senior Jewish court officers, was perceived as a provocation, which explains the first riot in 1355 in Toledo when the troops of Enrique II—who opposed the accession of Enrique's half-brother Pedro I to the throne of his father, Alfonso—launched an attack against the Jewish quarters of the city. Jews who had taken the side of 'Pedro the Jew' in this fratricidal struggle—his brother had in fact accused him of being the bastard of the queen and a Jewish convert by the name of Pero Gil—against Enrique Trastamara were the object of reprisals; eight thousand of them died in these massacres. When Enrique's yoke weighed even heavier on the survivors, conversions, which had formerly been individual affairs, now became collective and massive."

"Did the prophecies of Ferran Martinez play a role in this antisemitism?"

"They clearly did, for this Dominican—who was the confessor of the Queen Mother, Leonora, and who was also the archdeacon of Ecija—had begun voicing his imprecations in Seville in 1378. Comparing himself to the prophets of Israel, he sought to stir up *la gente menuda*, the common people, against the Jews. He called them the devil's disciples, symbols of greed and faithlessness, even though he was reprimanded and threatened with excommunication on several occasions."

"How did things go for the Jews of Cuenca?" I asked anxiously.

"Listen, it's very sad to say, but in Cuenca it was the town councilors themselves who sounded the alarm and called the populace to launch the assault against the *judería*, to pillage the quarter and forcibly convert its inhabitants.[3] No one really knows whether the chief rabbi of Castile, Salomon Halevi, converted before or after these riots. Taking the name of Pablo de Santa Maria, he became the bishop of Burgos. Many followed his lead, and from then on there were no longer any Jews in Cuenca. A new category, *conversos*, or new Christians, appeared, and from the outset they announced their hostility toward their former fellow believers."

"What proof is there in support of such claims?"

"The archives of the diocese of Cuenca show traces of a suit brought by Maria Rodriguez Mexia before the municipal court in 1408. She claimed from King Juan II the sum of five thousand maravedis a year that the Jewish community of Cuenca was required to pay her mother, Doña Teresa Gomez de Albornoz, whose single heiress she was, according to a concession granted by Enrique II and confirmed by Juan II and Enrique III. Since the town council had taken up arms to destroy and pillage the Jewish quarter and forcibly convert its inhabitants to Christianity, Maria Rodriguez claimed that the council ought to make restitution, that is, pay her the sum that represented the cumulative value of the lost tax over the previous twenty years."[4]

"That would mean that the pogroms against the Jews of Cuenca were earlier than those in Seville?"

"They probably occurred in 1388, or three years before the firing of the Toledo judería," my informant told me. "It was also during this desolate period that the grandparents of Joseph Hacohen, the Cohanim, fleeing the rule of the oppressor, left the town of Cuenca and took refuge in the fortress of Huete, where they were safe. In 1427 the collector of Jewish taxes found no one on whom to levy them, and the following year the town council confirmed that there was no longer a Jewish population. In 1441 Francisco Nuñez of Toledo in turn sent an emissary to collect the tax, but the council replied that it was well known that for quite some time there had been no Jews resident in the town of Cuenca."

What more did Abba want me to remember?

Still in conversation with my guide along the ancient ramparts of

Cuenca, we had arrived before the episcopal palace. Fernando then suggested that I visit it and introduced me to Don Dimaz Perez Ramirez, the director of the archives of the Inquisition that are kept there.

The Inquisition's tribunal, initially established in the present priory, was transferred by the inquisitor general, Don Gaspar de Quiroga, bishop of Cuenca, to Calle San Pedro in 1574, and then in 1583 to the town fortress. It remained there until 1808, the year in which the French occupied the town, established their head-quarters there, and partially destroyed the archives in order to heat the rooms. As for the origin of the Cuenca tribunal, opinions vary: some believe that in the beginning it was associated with the one in Murcia, from which it was separated in 1513, others that it was set up in Sigüenza only to be transferred to Cuenca—unless it was established in the capitals of two dioceses that then merged. All historians nevertheless agree in recognizing that in 1498 there was an inquisitorial tribunal in Cuenca acting with full independence.

Don Dimaz Perez Ramirez authorized me to plunge into the precious manuscripts with their enigmatic calligraphy penned in dark, wine-colored ink in an effort to find a trace of my ancestors. Thus I learned that the first inquisitorial edict had been proclaimed in the cathedral of Cuenca in 1489: the suspects had a grace period of thirty to forty days to confess their crimes. The isolation of the town and, at the same time, its relative proximity to Madrid explained the Inquisition's intense activity there; documentation from more than 480 lawsuits brought against moriscos in 1515 and 1630 are conserved in the diocesan archives, a figure higher than that for cases against those suspected of practicing Judaism. Penalties for the latter were, however, more severe than those for moriscos: *relajación, reconciliación*, the confiscation of goods, *abjuratio de levi* or *de vehementi*. There had been no Jews in Cuenca for a long time, and so the first inquisitors—Francisco Florez, archdeacon of Trastamara, and Bartolomé Gumiel, vicar general of the bishopric of Burgos—whom Queen Isabella had recommended the citizens of Cuenca to receive *benigne y amorosamente*, cordially and respectfully, fell on the *conver-*

sos, the new Christians, the *malos cristianos, sospechosos en la fé*, accused of practicing the Jewish faith in secret.

I went through the list of "crimes" that the Inquisition had drawn up: antireligious speech, suspect and unseemly speech, sorcery, superstition, fornication, blasphemy, heretical talk, false witness, being of Jewish descent, practicing Judaism. I was surprised to find no trace of Hebrew family names: to all appearances, when the majority of Jews had been forced to convert during the riots of 1388, they found themselves unilaterally assigned new first names, preferentially chosen from Christian martyrology so as not to raise any doubts as to their origin. They also had to choose a surname, whether by borrowing another family name, sometimes a famous one, or by taking the name of an animal, a trade, or even the town, village, or region they were from.

If Cuenca were definitively not a Hebrew patronym, could it be the case that Abba had wanted to change his name in order to erase the forced baptism, to forget the land of Sepharad?

Don Dimaz Perez Ramirez confirmed that there was no longer any trace in Cuenca of the ancient *sinoga*, as it was called in the Middle Ages, tucked away in the very center of the Jewish neighborhood in the Alcazar quarter. In 1403, in fact, the bishop Don Juan Cabeza de Vaca had transformed it into the parish church of Santa Maria la Nueva for the use of converts. Thus the newly converted Jews, the Guadalajaras, the Perez, the Sanchez of Teruel, the Montemayors, the Cañizares, were forced to participate in Christian worship on the very sites where they had performed their Jewish devotions.

Juan Cuenca, my ancestor, could thus not even console himself by reading the angular letters of *Yadekha u-berakhekha, elohekha natan*, for the Inquisition had taken care on its arrival to cover these Hebrew inscriptions with whitewash. Fragments of the Mudejar frieze from the mid-fourteenth century, quite similar to that from the Transito synagogue in Toledo, are still preserved at the bishop's palace, and, reviving my memories from Hebrew classes, I succeeded in deciphering this verse: "The Lord will ordain blessings for you upon your barns and upon all your undertakings. He will bless you in the land that the Lord your God is giving you."[5]

There was no longer a *sinoga* in Cuenca, but, Juanito, there is no doubt that you used to go to the home of Pedro Xuarez de Toledo, in Calle Pellejeria, who, just like Symuel Abenxuxe, was devoted to keeping the ancient law of Moses and hope in the messiah alive within you. You went there at the risk of your life, for when they saw the mules tied up in front of this house, the *malsines* would rush to denounce you to the inquisitors.

On 1 November 1478 the Catholic rulers had obtained from Pope Sixtus IV the bull Exigit Sincerae Devotionis, which authorized them to appoint an Inquisition in their kingdoms in order to prosecute heretical Christians, those converts suspected in the eyes of the inquisitors of practicing Jewish rites. On the model of Mohammed's mount, Al-Burak, which was neither horse nor mule, neither male nor female, they were called *alboraykos, tornadizos,* and *marranos,* this last term derived from *marrar,* which means "lacking in," or even from Arabic *mahram,* "forbidden," which was translated as "pork," the eating of which was forbidden to Jews just as much as it was to Muslims. It was time to put an end to conflicts between those who were also called *cristianos nuevos*—even when they were six generations distant from conversion!—as opposed to *cristianos viejos,* who were *lindos, limpios,* or "people of the nation," indeed of *la raza.* Thus can we understand the two measures adopted by the Inquisition in 1480: the segregation of Jews to distance them from converts, and the creation of a special tribunal to punish those secretly practicing Judaism. Could the idea of the Inquisition have been born in a *converso* environment, as Americo Castro and Sancho Albornoz think?

There was no longer a synagogue, but in the course of these secret *conventiculos* that replaced the teaching of the rabbis, you learned, Juanito, that candles were lit Friday evening and allowed to burn until the end of Sabbath, that you put on clean clothes at that time, that you fasted on Yom Kippur. You still knew the prayers and you recited them in Hebrew. Your sons, at birth, were circumcised—the Inquisition did not begin to inspect foreskins until 1635—and you gave them secret Hebrew first names. After their baptism you immersed them in lustral water to purify them, and on the seventh day after birth you poured gold, silver, pearls, wheat, and barley into their basins of worked copper so that they would be supplied with all these goods in this world. When one of yours died, you knew that you had to shave his beard, armpits, and others parts of the body, and your wife María piously preserved new shrouds in her cupboard for such occasions. You would make a pillow of virgin earth for the dead man, you would place a pearl and a coin in his mouth, and would turn the head to the wall. Your wife would sprinkle water so that the soul of the deceased might depart in peace, and you, Juanito, you would abstain from eating meat for three days as a sign of mourning, but you would make up for it during Lent after having made sure that the animal had been ritually slaughtered and that it had been marinated in salted water. You knew that you did not have the right to eat *tocino, liebre*, nor *conejo*, nor *peshkado liso*, and you were crazy about *pan senzeno* which you laid in for Passover.[6] You placed your hand, fingers outspread, on the head of your sons. You still knew all that, thanks no doubt to the physician Symuel Abenxuxe or Pedro Xuarez de Toledo, your masters.

Juanito, I know that Maria threw pellets of the dough she kneaded into the fire, and you for your part did not hesitate to ask for alms from a stranger in order to have oil for the synagogue. She kept her nail clippings so that they could be put in her grave—Is not she who burns them devout? Is not she who keeps them just, whereas she who throws them out is bad?[7]—and you, you demanded that only your own children wrap you in your shroud at the moment of death and that they place a lit candle in a saucer of water. You even forbade them to go to confession for fear that they would reveal your practices. You still knew all that, but your torturers knew it too! The manual of Eymerich, the efficient inquisitor from Aragon, the *Directorium inquisitorum*, had been in circulation since 1376 and provided details on various procedures, including those that allowed practitioners of Judaism to be recognized. Was it not this same Eymerich who burned Nicolas de Calabre, the relapsed, recidivist heretic who maintained that his master, Martin Gonsalvo de Cuenca—one of your ancestors perhaps—was the son of God, destined to live eternally, to convert the world, and to pray on Judgment Day for all the dead whom he would thus save from hell?[8]

However, you were dead and buried in 1490, Juanito, the year of your trial. But, provided there was enough proof—three testimonies, for example—the Inquisition could not only bring an action against a dead person but, even more, could "discharge" him, a euphemism masking the hypocrisy of the inquisitors who, cowardly to the point of not dirtying their own hands, referred the death sentence to the secular authority. Your kin were invited to take on your case if they so wished, by announcing an evidentiary search in the parish and posting it on the cathedral door. But by the end of the thirty-day period, clearly in no great hurry to defend your memory, none of them had come forward. But then they too were guilty of rebelling against the Church and were subject to having their property confiscated by the king. None of your descendants, none of those whom you cherished and blessed, had the courage to speak up against this posthumous trial, Juanito, there was no one to refute these attacks *contra fama y memoria*. One has to believe that you were seriously culpable, *pertinaz*, one of the stubborn ones. Had not your own sons been witnesses to your return to Judaism? Had you not replied in the affirmative to those of your companions who had proposed that you perform *tevila*? Did they not undress you, plunge you into the water of the Huecar while uttering the formula *baal teshuvah*, rub you with sand to cleanse the parts of your body that had received the holy chrism when you had been baptized? You were gravely suspect, your case was desperate, your descendants took fright and fled far from Cuenca. You had a court-appointed defender; the trial was held behind closed doors. Finally, the sentence was delivered: handed over to the secular arm.

A bull from Pope Innocent VIII on 15 June 1486 had authorized the inquisitors to proceed with the disinterment of corpses. This is what happened to you, Juanito: after having dried your remains to remove the smell of corruption, they were enclosed in a coffer decorated with dancing flames encircling your name painted in large letters, so that the crowd could follow the spectacle. On the *cadalso*, or platform, between two tiered rows of seats, *tablados*, intended for the judges and the accused, your effigy was set up, it too bearing your name.

The auto-da-fé had been announced a long time in advance, and it was market day on the Plaza Mayor. A dense, excited crowd had gathered to witness the event. You were hooted and jeered at before being burned. After that, at least you no longer risked contaminating your Christian neighbors—the Jewish cemetery over by the Tiradores had long since disappeared—and your sinning soul was saved, for does not fire purify all? Your property was confiscated along with that of your descendants to the second generation in the paternal line. Your house was leveled. Your prior death had at least spared you the water torture, the rack, the garrote, the wearing of the *sanbenito*, but not public shaming. Your ashes were scattered by the executioner so that no trace or memory of you would remain.[9] Who had denounced you?

The example of your trial did not, however, succeed in discouraging Joan de Cuenca, your grandson and an innkeeper by trade, a fugitive at the time of your trial, from renouncing his faith and its ancestral practices. This ancestor, for his part, was absolved in 1492, while still alive, but he was obliged to take the path of permanent exile immediately after his absolution for fear of a fresh condemnation.

You would have been in your thirties, Joancho, tall, thin, with a fair complexion and great dark eyes staring out from your face, curly hair that you wore long, and you were so very much alive that you passionately wanted to stay that way. At the beginning you didn't know what to reveal, what sin to confess to. You knew that in the neighboring village of Huete, malicious witnesses had accused monks of having sent oil for use in the synagogue, monks like Alonso de Madrid, the curate of Peraleja, who was condemned then absolved in 1492. Or that other one, Diego Gonzalez de Madrid, curate of San Nicolas of Huete, accused in 1490 of passing himself off as a rabbi by procuring a letter of recommendation from Abraham Senior, the chief rabbi of Castile, with the sole purpose of gaining a few maravedis. The sentence, sent down in 1491, found him guilty of crimes punishable by major excommunication, confiscated his property, and turned him over to the civil authorities. You had probably heard of the trial of Leonor Garcia, again from Huete, a *reconciliada*, charged in February 1491 with having been prompted by the crypto-Jewess Juana Gonzalez to fast on Yom Kippur. Diego de Cuenca, also originally from Huete, had, for his part, asked for a revision of the sentence pronounced against his mother, who was already dead, by challenging the false testimony of the laundress Susana, the *hermosa hembra*.

Imprisoned, with the list of your property drawn up, you reflected on your situation. The prosecutor, at the first arraignment, informed you of his intention to accuse you, as a convert, of following Jewish precepts. They threatened you, once they had determined the place and date of your return to Judaism, with removing the assets that you had when you began to follow Jewish practices from the list of your possessions that had been made the day of your arrest; the other assets would remain confiscated. You had to confess, tell the truth not only as concerned yourself but also denounce your accomplices. They pointed out the seriousness of your crime while assuring you that if you confessed, the inquisitors would view your case with some compassion, more precisely, that they would spare you from torture. For the moment you were simply *sospechoso*, somewhat suspect. You had to avoid being convicted of *abjuratio de levi*, for which you risked a canonical reprimand, admonition, recanting; with a conviction of *abjuratio de vehementi*, you would incur supplementary punishment; and with *suspectus violenter*, it would mean imprisonment. If they succeeded in establishing proof of your crimes, you would become *convencido o probado*: in addition to recanting in public and wearing the *sanbenito*, you would incur life imprisonment. The inquisitors also distinguished the obstinate or recalcitrant, and the recidivists or *relapsos*.

The *audiencia de la carcel*—distinct from that which would later take place in the courtroom, the *audiencia publica o continua*—was held in the prison itself, in the absence of the defense. The tribunal and the prosecutor worked in concert to force you to confess your errors. This was the best way to inculpate you. On the other hand, a false confession might send you to the torture chamber. If you denied the prosecution's charges, the judge would pass a provisional sentence and ask that proof be supplied. You and your defense would receive a copy, but it would be so cleverly phrased that it would be impossible for you to recognize the witnesses. You would have the advantage of a reprieve of three days to reflect. You could challenge the charges in the accusation and submit a questionnaire, requesting that witnesses for the defense be interrogated. Then would come the *sentencia de prueba*, for which the witnesses would have to take an oath. After the hearing of witnesses for the prosecution, who were anonymous, for fear of reprisals—it might be a matter of close relatives, your children perhaps, informers, themselves often former converts—and the hearing of witnesses for the defense, you waited for the verdict, which was turned over to specialists. A date was set for this.

You benefited from a grace period of forty days to confess, and if it were judged that your admission had been made in good faith and was complete, which assumed that the tribunal had not assembled other compromising materials coming from another source, your trial would be waived. You would nonetheless have to expiate your sin and participate in the auto-da-fé. On the other hand, if you omitted information about all those who had participated with you in "Mosaic practices," your confession would only inculpate you more seriously.

When the inquisitors, clever as they were, asked you, Joancho, the question: "Do you believe that Christ was born of a virgin?" you could have pretended to be stupid, not to be feeling well. You could have stalled like others had done before you: "What a great example the Virgin gives us!" You could have thrown the question back: "And you, do you believe it?" You could have feigned surprise: "Why do you ask me that? I am a Christian!" You cleverly replied: "I am weak and ignorant, I don't know any theology. Don't ask me questions like that."[10]

They accused you of not crossing yourself, of not going to mass or of going only because you distrusted your neighbors and so as not to be excommunicated, of not going to confession, of working on Sunday, of avoiding saying the name of Jesus, of slandering the Virgin Mary and Christianity, of eating lamb at Easter, of celebrating the baptism of your newly born only in private, refusing any church ceremony: in short, you were accused of transgressions against Christianity. But they did not succeed in proving that you had returned to the religion of your ancestors or that you observed the *mitsvot*.

There was little doubt that you had to observe great precautions, dissimulate continuously. In order to respect the Sabbath, you had to leave the town and go afield, unless you suddenly fell ill Friday evening. At times you employed a ruse, having a Christian servant look after the inn that you ran. Your wife, Isabel, when she paid a visit to her family, always took care to bring along her distaff and spindles to make everyone think that she had worked the whole day. If any visitor dropped in unexpected on a Friday evening, you had to rush the dish of Sabbath meat out of sight and replace it with fish that you had also prepared the day before. On the other hand, certain holy days were just too risky; then you had to make do, with a heavy heart, by celebrating them in your inner temple, Joancho. They could wring no confession from you and no accusation, no deposition by witnesses ever succeeded in convicting you of heresy. You were acquitted.

You avoided the *quemadero*, as well as the "wall," life imprisonment, but you had to be present, as proof of your good faith and for your edification, at the public auto-da-fé of your companions in misfortune, jeered, whipped in public, paraded through the town in bare feet, stripped to the waist, bearing the insignia of their offense, while the town crier proclaimed their sentences.

The mayor at my side, I undertook to trace the itinerary of those condemned by the Inquisition in Cuenca. The ceremony was initiated at dawn, in public, on the Plaza Mayor. The condemned left the *castillo* that looks down on the town, of which only an archway remains. A procession consisting of the clergy was preceded by the great banner of the Inquisition. Those who had recanted *de vehementi* had to hold lighted candles and wear the *sanbenito*. They passed barefoot before the Carmelite convent and the parish church of San Pedro, where Isabel Herraiz is buried, condemned for illuminism, a form of spirituality the Church distrusted. Then they went down

Calle San Pedro to the Plaza Mayor and the cathedral that houses the tombs of the Montemayors, prominent rich Jewish converts. Earlier their remains had rested in the synagogue. It was on this square or in front of the principal façade of the monastery of San Pablo, whose Dominicans were empowered by the Holy Office, that the autos-da-fé were celebrated. The condemned then were led along the wall of the episcopal palace. They reached Plaza de la Merced, the oldest part of the Jewish quarter, then finally the Campo de San Francisco, the execution site for prisoners that the Inquisition had turned over to the secular arm. Today it is occupied by the Deputación Provincial.

You were acquitted, Joancho, but nonetheless not proven innocent. They had simply not assembled enough proof against you. To declare you innocent would, in fact, have given you an advantage in the event of a fresh accusation. Your ancestors had already been exiled from Jerusalem, Joancho, but they had not fled Spain, neither in 1338 on the occasion of the *matanzas* nor in 1453 when Constantinople was captured, which some interpreted as announcing the arrival of the Messiah. Spain—one of the last Christian countries to expel its Jews, once the Reconquest had been completed and there was no longer any need for the "treasure," the source of funding that they represented—was turned over to Torquemada, *bestya kon figura de benadam*. And thus, the first day of the fifth month of the year 1492, the first of Adar, King Ferdinand, on the advice of his spouse, decided to banish the Jews within the three-month period between the ninth of Iyyar and the ninth of Av. The converts had, in fact, protested that it would be impossible for them to be perfect, sincere Christians as long as there were still Jews among them in Spain. Under the influence of the Catholic clergy, Isabella—although she had intervened on 7 July 1477 in Trujillo to take the Jewish *aljama* under her protection and forbid all aggression and harassment against its inhabitants: *Todos los judios de mis reiños son mios y estan so mi proteccion y amparo, y a mi pertenece de los defender y amparar y mantener en justicia* (All the Jews of my kingdoms belong to me and are under my protection; it is my responsibility to protect them and defend them and to ensure justice)[11]—became the enemy of Israel, going so far as to accuse her husband of having Jewish blood: "They married me to you so that you would lend them strength and support."[12]

Torquemada had drafted one of the three versions of the decree: "We order and command all men and women, old and young, who glorify the name of Israel and who live and reside under our government, to go into exile, to leave all the regions where they dwell, to abandon the cities of our kingdom and to betake themselves to another country within the space of three months from the first of May to the end of the month of July." Offenders would incur the penalty of death by hanging or of forced conversion. On the other hand, those who in the course of these three months converted to Christianity would be allowed to stay where they were, retain their fortunes and their property, and would be exempt from all taxes and all constraint; the Inquisition, moreover, promised not to reopen inquiries into their affairs for ten years. "For purposes of control, we enjoin everyone, princes, great lords, and judges of all provinces and cities, to affix the royal emblem called in Spanish *señal real* to the entry of every Jewish house in every place where these reside."[13]

Three months to leave everything. You traded your inn, Joancho, for a mule, your vineyard for a few mattresses, and you set out with your wife, Isabel, for Cartagena in the heat of August, on the 16th of the month of Av, in one of sixteen large ships loaded with livestock. Like a child hurrying to school, you carried, pressed to your heart, only your Torah, the law of your God. To take courage, you and Isabel sang and played the tambourine.

"How many of them left?" I ventured.
"Fifty, sixty thousand?" Don Dimaz Perez Ramirez replied. Abravanel puts forward the figure of 300,000; the demographers, 70,000 to 120,000. At most 200,000, asserts the historian Luis Suarez Fernandez, or some 30,000 families from Castile, the ultimate place of refuge for the 216 *aljamas* in Christian Spain.
"No one intervened on their behalf?" I asked in surprise.
"Don Isaac Abravanel and Don Abraham Senior tried to save them, Abravanel even offering a considerable sum to have the edict

of exile revoked. This is when Torquemada intervened. Brandishing a crucifix, he cried out: "Judas sold Christ for thirty pieces of silver. Your Majesties wish to sell him for thirty thousand ducats. Well then, here he is; sell him!" Despite the brilliant pleading of the great Jewish scholars, the king and queen replied: "Enough, speak no more of this to us!" The queen promised to convert all the communities of Spain by force if Don Abraham Senior refused to apostatize. In order to save a great number of Jews from sin, the latter embraced Christianity despite himself, but Jews converted by the thousands and some, who were already on their way, even turned back on their tracks in the face of the tribulations and suffering that they met and finally apostatized.

I knew that these exiles had fled wherever the wind took them: to Africa, Asia, Greece, Turkey. Their journeys were strings of misfortune and maltreatment inflicted by Genoese sailors and Muslims who did not hesitate to disembowel some fugitives, in order to recover the gold that they had swallowed for safekeeping, and to drown others, when plague and hunger did not decimate them, when they were not abandoned on desert islands by lawless, godless captains, or when they were not sold like animals.

Some of the exiles from Cuenca, including my ancestors Joancho and Isabel, retained the name of their town of origin as a family name in the Ottoman Empire. Sultan Bayezid II received them eagerly with these words: "Can you call such a ruler [Ferdinand] intelligent and wise? He impoverishes his country and enriches mine!"[14]

Bernard Lazare's "The Cosmopolitan's Letter" haunted me even more: was Spain our homeland, the land where we had loved?

II

Into the Lands of the Grand Turk

Ande ir en galut?
En las tyerras del Grande Turco.

Where to go into exile?
Into the lands of the Grand Turk.

Joancho and Isabel—obeying the injunction "Oh Israel, why do you sleep? Rise up and leave this cursed country forever" of Rabbi Isaac Zarfati, who invited his fellow believers to join him in the Ottoman Empire, a land of abundance where they could find peace, acquire property, and be free to dress as they wished[1]—thus arrived in the lands of the Grand Turk in 1492 as part of the first wave of immigration, with twelve thousand other families fleeing the persecution of Spain. *Kendi gelen*, arriving of their own free will, they found various Jewish communities already there: Romaniot,[2] Greek speaking, Rabbanite, and Karaite—those who did not recognize the authority of the Oral Law. Among them, many had been deported—*sürgünlü*—for Sultan Mehmed II had undertaken to repopulate the deserted city when Constantinople had been taken in 1453. Shortly after arriving from Spain, they reconstituted their communities, the *kehilot*, on the model of their older Castilian *fuero*.

Your ways and customs, even your language rapidly put a stamp on your surroundings. In addition to your baptismal name and the name of your town of origin, you had also carried with you, Joancho and Isabel, Castilian, the language in which all your business would henceforth be done in the cities of Salonika, Constantinople, Cairo, and Venice. But why Spanish? Shouldn't the ancestral language of the Jews have been Hebrew? Driven from Spain, should the Sephardim not have returned to their original language? We must conclude that even if Jews continued to pray in Hebrew, once the multitude of heretical books and "false" Bibles had been burned in the public square of Toledo, only a cultivated minority continued to speak it in the kingdom of Castile at the close of the sixteenth century.

"You know the value I attach to language, even more than to race," wrote Miguel de Unamuno, the poet and rector of the University of Salamanca.[3] Preserving Spanish—was this not a way of indicating the close spiritual kinship, so much closer than race and blood, between the Jewish and Spanish peoples? "A woman must abandon the house of her father," continued Miguel de Unamuno: accordingly, the Jews of Spain would have abandoned Hebrew to be married to Spanish. Could it be that, instead of Spain, *djudyo* had become your only true homeland? Did the persistence of Judeo-Spanish over centuries not demonstrate that the eastern Sephardim had pardoned, even long forgotten, the persecutions that they suffered in Spain, in that Spain of which Yehuda Leib Gordon bitterly noted in 1808 that it had not been punished for the infamous treatment inflicted on its Jews?[4]

By making Spain one of the homelands where the Jews had loved, Bernard Lazare seemed to share the opinion of Max Nordau according to which it was time to "reset the clocks and think of the past as past."[5] In the course of a cruise on the Danube on 24 August 1903 that took Senator Pulido and his family from Belgrade to Orsova, they heard an elderly couple on the bridge speaking an "incorrect Castilian" and immediately deduced that they were Spanish Jews who had preserved during four centuries of exile the cult of "Spain, our dear mother country."[6] Impressed by this love of the Spanish land, Senator Pulido from then on tirelessly lobbied the Spanish government for the protection of the Castilian language in the Orient, extolling reconciliation between Spaniards and Sephardim.

Joancho and Isabel, did you speak Spanish out of sentimentality or because you did not know any other language? Did you still speak only Spanish, or simply "Jewish"—*djudyo*—as you called it among yourselves? Supreme irony, Spain that was so proud, so attentive to the purity of its blood, seemed entirely corrupted by Jewish and marrano blood, to the point that, in France, *espagnol* and *marrano* came to be synonymous, just like *portugais* and *juif* ("Jew") later on.

In Madrid, a week earlier, on Calle del Pintor Rozalès, I had seen the extent of astonishment that my broken, archaic Spanish aroused. As a child, without knowing it I had learned the Judeo-Spanish that my parents had resorted to when they didn't want me to understand. Ima had the habit of recounting her marital woes in endless telephone conversations with her sisters. I would slip under the telephone table, the other earpiece in my hand, which never failed to exasperate Ima, who would then switch to her mother tongue. Abba and Ima also used it to criticize others or to situate their affinity. *Son de los muestros, este es de mi pueblo*, Abba would decree after a rapid glance around the restaurant. By way of confirmation of his "intuition," he would take the first opportunity to prove his hunch by slipping the fateful question to the party under observation: *sos de la grande michpaha?* I never caught him making an error in this little game. And his childish joy when a confirmation came from the person he had addressed: *Es dyudyo! i de Stambol!* Thus the first words of this unknown language were words of complaint, suffering, recognition, or mockery. My maternal grandparents spoke to me in Judeo-Spanish, but I always replied in French, as if out of modesty or embarrassment.

If I hit myself, the consoling words *Ay de mi!* came to my lips. If I were giving an account of something surprising, in order that others share my wonder: *Asi bivas tu!* Similarly, if I were sick with some childhood illness, so that others would suffer along with me. At times, I forced myself to sneeze three times in a row to be sure I would garner the anguished response: *bivas, kreskas, i grandeskas!* Or even *kon salud i kon vida!* If I choked on something: *oras klaras, oras buenas!* If some childish worry troubled me, people would wish me: *tus ojos no veyan mal*, maybe even *kyen mal te kere?* If I had said something that seemed relevant, *tu boka koma myel*. If someone complimented me on how good I was looking, they repeated the words of exorcism against the evil eye: *el Dyo ke te eskape de ojo malo i de ayin ara!* or this phrase *ojo malo, avla mala, ayin ara ke no mos toke*. If I were going off to summer camp: *kaminos de letche i myel!* When I came back with rosy cheeks, I was greeted with *manzanikas koloradas, las ke vyenen de Stambol*. On the other hand, if I pestered the adults too much, there came the supreme reproach: *ya basta, ija de un mamzer!*

Later, after or before reading the *Memoirs* of Canetti, I asked my polyglot father: "What is your mother tongue?" He replied, "At home, it was Judeo-Spanish; in the street with my buddies, Greek and Armenian; with the servants, Turkish; at school, French; with the governess, English; at the *Gymnasium*, German." He also thought that he spoke Italian, but in fact it was an astonishing hodge-podge which, however, worked very well, especially when it was accompanied by bobbing, weaving, and mimicry that charmed me as much as it infuriated his wife, who found him decidedly "too Eastern" and superstitious: no hats on the bed, it was a sign of death; no cupboards left open, for fear of dispute in the house. If salt were spilled at the table, a pinch of it had to be immediately thrown over each shoulder to counter bad luck. If a button were sewn or a hem fixed on a dress that someone was wearing, you cried out: *En riva de kyen kuzgo? En riva de la ija de el Rey de Fransa. Eya tenga tus ansyas, i tu sus ganansyas!* If your mother, wife, or daughter were sick, you pretended to tear out your hair, Abba, sighing noisily, *Aman, aman, aman!* Mercy! what is to become of me? It was precisely this "too much," this overdoing that I adored, that I received as a precious heritage.

The period from the end of the fifteenth to the end of the sixteenth century was a brilliant one for the Jews at court. They put their international connections at the sultan's disposal, turned themselves into sources of information for the Sublime Porte, became moneychangers, moneylenders, and physicians once again, developed wool and leather industries, and set up printing presses. The law of Islam had granted you, Joancho, Isabel, the status of protected residents, or *dhimmi*, as in Muslim Spain, but it also subjected you to the *djizya* or *kharadj*, to a head tax, and you were not authorized to testify against any Muslim. The height of houses, the type and color of clothes were, once again, the object of strict regulation, as well as the mounts you rode on.[7] New curses were not long in striking you: crushed by levies and taxes, soon you had to cede your place to Greeks and Armenians. Innumerable fires periodically ravaged your residences, and in addition you met competition from Europe and from Smyrna. Smyrna: ruled by one exalted individual, Sabbatai Zevi, who, after having been made a rabbi at the age of eighteen, nonetheless gave himself over to totally irreligious conduct, not hesitating, for example, to forbid ritual fasting, to recommend the consumption of forbidden foods, or even to pronounce the tetragrammaton. Expelled in 1651 by the Smyrna rabbinate, he then wandered in Greece and Turkey, sowing disorder and confusion by prophesying the imminent deposition of the sultan, the return of the ten lost tribes of the kingdom of Israel that had been deported to Assyria, and unilaterally proclaiming himself the Messiah. Arrested by the Turks and ordered to chose between conversion to Islam and death, he opted in 1666 for conversion. Even if dozens of thousands of his disconcerted faithful returned to Judaism, many of his congregation followed his example and apostatized, creating the sect of the *Dönme*. Established in 1683 in Salonika, a number of them became leaders in the Young Turk movement in 1909.

I

Varna: "Cuenca Brothers"

After Jacob's death I found countless albums with photographs of this extended family that had dispersed around the world. The oldest photographs, showing Yako Cuenca in Varna, dated from the beginning of the twentieth century. Varna, a major port on the Black Sea that would be renamed Stalin in 1949, had three hundred Jewish residents in 1880 and fifteen hundred in 1919. In addition to the Sephardim there was also a small Ashkenazic community, and the Alliance Israélite Universelle had opened an elementary school there in 1880 and, somewhat later, two vocational schools.

Yako Cuenca, one of the distant descendants of Joancho the innkeeper, had taken Vida de Botton as his wife. Their seven children were born in Constantinople: four sons, Joseph, Salomon, my paternal grandfather Meier, and David. Three daughters also blessed this union: Sarina, Élise, Fortunée. But the good Yako, instead of laying down the law on the model of Yako Balta,[1] was no match for his circumstances and lived from hand to mouth. He never worked a day in his life, and his only economic activity consisted of renting part of his house to a maker of pomade for stiffening mustaches! The family was continuously in financial trouble, and so the eldest son, Joseph, had to go to work very early, taking humble jobs such as moneychanger or shop clerk. Joseph was so poor that to get to the store he even had to go around the Golden Horn on foot, which represented about three or four hours of walking. But Joseph was clever: he made a deal with a ferryman who agreed to take him across every workday, provided that Joseph would come and row on his days off.

Subsequently, Joseph found employment in Bulgaria, in Varna. There he sold small packages of cigarette paper. Competition was fierce for poor Joseph, since he had to get to the village before the others, over bad roads where his sleigh was also in danger of being attacked by wolves! His employers were very satisfied with his service, but they were getting old, so he made them an offer: "I will continue to work for you throughout the region, but if I succeed in saving a certain amount, you will sell me your business." The figure Joseph named was a colossal amount, so that his employers, thinking that he would never succeed in getting it together, all the more willingly agreed. Now, it had happened that Joseph took as his wife Rika Covo, the granddaughter of Avraham Yitschak Covo, who was originally from Ruse (Rustchuk), like Elias Canetti, a distant relative who devoted a book to his community.[2] Joseph received a generous dowry and was thus able to buy the business from his employers.

Joseph was very devout: he went to the synagogue every day, and Friday evening on returning home he never failed to wish all his family *semanadas buenas i claras, shabat shalom.* Of his brother Meier, on the other hand, people said: *beza mezuza i arova pita!* During this time, back in Constantinople, Joseph's family continued to experience difficulties. As the eldest brother, Joseph felt responsible. He took in hand two of his brothers: David, whom he sent away to an Ashkenazic school where he learned dyeing and German, and Meier, who found work with a grain merchant before leaving for Cologne, where he later established a business in printing supplies, starting with linotype then moving on to offset printing. Salomon, the fourth brother, preferred to remain in Constantinople until the time when Joseph's business grew even bigger, and he too collaborated in running the cigarette paper factory.

It was in Varna that Salomon, Jacob's father, met Rebecca Nahmias, his future wife, and in Varna as well their eldest daughter, Vicky, was born in 1905. It was also in Varna that Victoria Nahmias, who had been born in Salonika in 1878 and was the half-sister of *Nona* Rebecca, married Haïm Pappo, who filled the office of rabbi in Haskovo and to whom she bore six sons. Haïm's elder brother, Lazare Pappo, also lived in Varna, with an equally large family. And it was in Varna that Jacques Policar, born in 1916 in Plovdiv as the grandson of Sultana Nahmias, another sister of Nona Rebecca, spent his holidays in the company of his uncles Jules, Ernesto, and Nisso.

The three Cuenca bothers, Joseph, David, and Salomon, decided one fine day to set up a ship chandler's business together in the port of Varna. An Englishman who worked for the British Intelligence Service introduced himself and offered to collaborate with them by providing information on the comings and goings of ships in the port, but the Cuenca brothers refused. The three brothers also sold arms—perhaps to Russian revolutionaries. Wasn't David in Odessa in 1906? A firing range was available for clients who wanted to try out their weapons, and one day a bullet passed so close to the temple of *Tsio* Meier that they decided to give this business up. After the persecution of the Greeks by the Bulgarians, Joseph worried that the Jews' turn would be next, so he sold his business in order to return to Constantinople where he began selling paper. As always, the business flourished in his hands and *Tsia* Rika was able each evening to take home the day's profit, little boxes of gold coin.

At the end of World War I many members of the Cuenca family left Constantinople to take up residence in Vienna. Austria seemed more "civilized" to them, but they were also fleeing the epidemics, Yako and Vida having both been carried off by an eczema-related fever in the 1920s.

Meier was the first to leave for Vienna in order to sound out the market. David and Joseph would soon join him. This was the birth of "Cuenca Brothers," the four brothers creating a family network.

Three of the four Cuenca brothers were so close that they formed other alliances among themselves, pushing endogamy to the point of marrying their own nieces, the daughters of their brothers. David, for example, married his niece Flora, the daughter of his older brother Joseph. She didn't even have to change her name. Of this union little Peppo was born in 1922, on the third floor of a building on Ausstellungsstrasse, not far from the great Ferris wheel at the Prater Park. Peppo then had to address as grandfather and grand-mother those who were also his uncle and aunt, who themselves had become the parents-in-law of their brother and brother-in-law. And his mama was the woman whom he could have called his cousin. Meier, the third brother, followed the example of his brother David and married Esther, the eldest daughter of his sister Sarina, herself the wife of Bohor Frances, the physician of Sultan Abdul Hamid in Bursa. With a single stroke his sister became his mother-in-law. With Esther Tsio Meier had two children who were also born in Istanbul: Jacky and Nelly. But they in turn had no cousin, since she was their mother. But the niece-spouse, the mother-cousin, was frail, and she died. When the snow came and spread a white carpet on her tomb, Tsio Meier married a second time, to Grete, a charming Viennese. Fortunée, the third of the Cuenca sisters, had only one daughter with Albert Benbassat, and was nothing more to her than a mother. As for Élise, the youngest of the Cuenca sisters, she first gave her husband Moïse Salti two sons, *maşallah*, then five daughters, two of whom perished in the crematoriums of Auschwitz.

Were the Cuenca brothers obeying Raphael's injunction to Tobias to take Sarah, the daughter of Raguel, to wife? "You, as next of kin to her, have before all other men a hereditary claim on her. . . . You have every right to take her in marriage. . . . Raguel can by no means keep her from you or promise her to another man without incurring the penalty of death according to the decree of the book of Moses. Indeed he knows that you, rather than any other man, are entitled to marry his daughter."[3] However, Leviticus codifies in very precise fashion the rules of conjugal union, and consequently forbids incest: "None of you shall come near anyone of his own flesh to uncover nakedness."⁴ This prohibition affects the father, mother, mother-in-law, sister, granddaughter, half-sister, aunt, uncle, daughter-in-law, sister-in-law, and the sister of one's wife as long as the wife is alive. The motive for such a prohibition is "immodesty," "infamy," "ignominy," "fouling," and those who transgress against these prohibitions are liable to being stoned, burned alive, subjected to the whip and *karet*.

> *Se paseava Silvana*
> *Por el verjel que tenia.*
> *Por ayi la oyo su padre.*
> *De altas torres, de ayi arriva.*
> *Ven aki tu Silvana,*
> *Ven aki tu ija mia.*
> *Ke bien arrelumbras Silvana*
> *Mejor de la reyna la madre tuya!*
> *De este modo de palavras*
> *De amores la aprometia.*
> *De sus ojos eya yorava,*
> *De su boca eya dezia:*
> *No lo kier el Dyo del sielo*
> *A ser combleza de la mi madre.*

> Silvana was strolling
> In her orchard.
> Her father heard her
> From high in his towers, and he came.
> "Come here, Silvana,
> Come here, my daughter,
> You are resplendent, Silvana,
> More ravishing than the queen, your mother!"
> Thus with words of love
> Her father embraced her.
> Her eyes wept
> And her mouth said:
> "God does not wish such a thing,
> That I should be the rival of my mother."⁵

Meier, David, perhaps you took justification from the Halakah, which, while prohibiting marriage between a brother and sister, an aunt and a nephew, does not prohibit it between an uncle and a niece.[6]

With the end of the Ottoman Empire and inflation, there was soon no longer any money to be made from business in Vienna. David, who in the meantime had worked in Belgium and then in Morocco, where he decorated the sultan's harem with mirrors—his patron offered him as recompense a sword set with precious stones—decided to set up a business near Paris, where he sold supplies for dairies. The family lived in an apartment in Enghien. Tsio Meier, Tsia Esther, and their two children, who had also chosen to keep the family together but could no longer pay for a residential hotel, came to join them. "I used to go to bed at night without knowing who I would wake up with the next morning," Peppo still remembers. Jacky played the big brother, bringing home pastries, giving his cousin Peppo a ride on the back of his bicycle, giving him his first driving lesson. But friction was inevitable in the small, crowded apartment.

Joseph, for his part, had settled in Nice, and he decided to set his daughter Flora up in business with the little money he had left. He had owned an apartment building in Vienna but the tenants had refused to allow themselves to be evicted, and his wife Rika had gambled away all her fortune at the casino in Nice. Flora gave her name to the shop, which is still there, in midtown. This clothes business was in near ruin until the day she discovered an employee stealing and selling the silk blouses that her clientele of navy wives from an American ship stationed at Villefranche were crazy about. David and his family once again left to join them. In Nice, David sold a pasteurization plant after a German had given him the formula for injecting chemicals into ham so as not to have to marinate it for days in brine. During the war, David took in many Spanish refugees in a building that he organized as a dormitory, feeding them on *garvansos*. Later a rich Egyptian Jew with communist sympathies made them the gift of a hilltop villa, La Lobélia, where they received refugees from Austria and Germany who had much greater needs. Peppo, who had voluntarily given up his morning bit of sugar to his grandparents, still remembers a little rhyme that he used to hum each day to take his mind off his hunger:

There's no more food in the house,
We'll just have to do without.
But we'd fill up, if we could turn up
A great big old turnip.

2

Salonika

Moïse and Allegra

Banished from Spain, Jews also chose Salonika, the "mother of Israel," as a destination, since it offered the persecuted Jews a refuge as sure as Jerusalem.[1]

The first wave of immigrants arrived immediately after the expulsion of 1492, not hesitating to sacrifice all their belongings in order to safeguard their faith. A second wave, this time of marranos, arrived in the sixteenth century. Brought up in the Christian religion, they still crossed themselves at times and uncovered their heads before holy objects. Conflict arose between these two communities, the former treating the latter as "offspring of goyim." After 1526, as a consequence of the campaigns of Suleiman the Magnificent in central Europe, Ashkenazim arrived from Austria, Transylvania, and Hungary. Lastly, Provençal Jews in Salonika summoned their fellow believers, expelled from Provence in 1550, to come and join them so that they too might live in "peace and security." In this way Salonika became a true Jewish city and remained so until its annexation by Greece in 1912, a city that counted no fewer than thirty-six distinct Jewish communities, where Spanish acquired such preponderance that Jews originating in other countries learned Castilian in their turn. The Jews reproduced the model of community organization of the Spanish *aljamas*, the statutes of which had been fixed by the synod of Valladolid in 1432.

Although families of modest means spoke only the Spanish of the age of Cervantes, at the Talmud Torah they studied Hebrew and Turkish, then the official language, since Salonika was still under Ottoman rule. In families that were better off, Castilian had been preserved, but they also spoke French, the mark of distinction in the social hierarchy. France was, in fact, the most esteemed of foreign nations, even if the merchants preferred Germany. In the course of a visit that he made in 1911 to Salonika, the sultan summoned several particularly deserving students to study in the prestigious French secondary school in Constantinople. However, Serbs, Croats, Bulgarians, and Montenegrins soon rose in revolt and were at the gates of Constantinople. The Balkan War broke out and all foreigners were sent away. Turkey collapsed, and Salonika became Greek: new laws and customs regulations were promulgated. European Turkey was cut up, part going to the Bulgarians and part to the Serbs.

All Jews clearly retained an emotional memory of Salonika before World War I, where the Sephardim, in the majority, claimed to live very harmoniously with the other minorities, Turks, Bulgarians, Greeks. Jews also benefited from the Statute of Capitulations signed in the time of François I and continuously renewed until then, and they enjoyed great autonomy within their own community. However, in 1923, Kemal Atatürk denounced the treaty, and thereafter the day for the compulsory closing of businesses was fixed as Sunday and no longer the Sabbath.

Family life, the affective relations among kin, family solidarity, the ritual celebration of holy days—these took first place. Thus, one would visit the deceased at the cemetery—*ir a ziyara*—to invite them to celebrate the new year. This was also the occasion to whitewash houses. People had a sense of hospitality: if someone arrived unannounced, he was well received and was traditionally offered the *charope blanko*, a glass of water and coffee on a silver platter. Each lady had her "day" for receiving, to share gossip and tea, and would host an impressive number of invitees in the most luxurious fashion possible. Certainly, ostentation counted for a great deal, but people also knew how to help one another and gave proof of community solidarity on the least occasion. Life was pleasant on the shores of the Bosphorus. People sailed in little boats, had cottages on the water.[2]

> *Si la mar era de letche,*
> *los barkitos de kanela* . . .
>
> If the sea were of milk,
> the little boats of cinnamon . . .[3]

It would seem that Jews hated Armenians, affecting a feeling of superiority with regard to them. The same Iberian pride was evident in relations with Ashkenazim, who were in a distinct minority and of much humbler status, not even having one synagogue among the thirty-seven in the city. Admittedly, the Greeks and Turks treated Jews as *çifut*; to be sure, there were fights and stone throwing on the Sabbath, and on Good Friday Jews did not dare to leave home, since the accusation of ritual murder was revived every year. But this was nothing in comparison to what the Jews of other cities such as Konya or Damascus had to suffer.[4]

But on the Good Friday of 28 April 1899, a Jew by the name of Joseph Avigdor, my great-grandfather on my mother's side, the father of *Mamu* Léa, who lived in Daghaman, a suburb of Constantinople, was attacked by Greeks in Tarabya, a municipality within the city of Istanbul on the shores of the Bosphorus. He had gone there neither to cure some bronchial ailment nor to breathe the fresh air and have a fish dinner with family, but for business, for, like the majority of Jews, he was a merchant. Some overexcited residents, made zealous by the account that they had heard in church of the agony of Christ, wanted to take their revenge on this Jew, the descendant, in their view, of deicides. Your father doubtless didn't dare tell you, Mamu, out of shame or modesty or perhaps to maintain his prestige in your child's eyes, how the police and then the administrator of the Greek community had to intervene to protect him from the vindictiveness of the crowd. He was then thirty-eight years old, and it was only when surrounded by gendarmes that he was able to embark safe and sound on a ship for his home shore.[5]

But it was only in the 1920s, with of the arrival in Salonika of Greeks from Asia Minor, who envied Jewish prosperity, that true antisemitism appeared. In 1922, Venizelos, a liberal leader, took power after suffering a first defeat at the hands of partisans of King Constantine in 1917. The *abalaï*, the subsequent exchange of Orthodox Christian populations from Asia Minor for Turks then transported to Anatolia, only aggravated the situation.

Prima Allegra, the granddaughter of Élise Cuenca—for whom her parents had still not chosen between the names Simha or Alice, until a year after her birth when a cousin imposed this compromise—was born in Salonika. Although she chose Abba, her first cousin, as her escort to her first ball, she married Moïse Akşiyote. According to him, Abba was a very good dancer, the life of the party, openhearted, happy-go-lucky. Why then did she prefer Moïse over him? After all, didn't Abba belong to the "royal family," as the Jews of Istanbul called them?

"I didn't want to marry a cousin," she said in justification.

But this was common practice in this family!

"And then he was thirteen years older than me. And Moïse was only eight . . ."

Primo Moïse, who considered himself *gueso ajeno*, the odd man out, was descended, it is true, from an illustrious line of physicians: his own father had been an army doctor; Peppo Akşiyote, the famous neurologist, had opened the first neurology clinic at the faculty of medicine at the University of Istanbul; Angelo Akşiyote had been the sultan's physician. But Moïse was disallowed by a quota imposed on Jewish students who wanted to study medicine; he was prevented from specializing in pediatrics, which was reserved for Muslims, and had to settle for becoming a surgeon and the head physician of the hospital. He remained bitter over this, even though he did not retire until 1985. After having liquidated all his property in Istanbul, including his summer house in the islands, he left in the company of Allegra to take up residence in Mexico with their children and grandchildren.

Moïse was the third of five siblings: Benjamin, Victor, Sol, and Annette, each more remarkable than the others, if one is to believe them. After meeting Sol, I discovered a song in honor of a heroine with the same name, "Sol la Sadika," whose distasteful torments and unhappy fate she fortunately did not share. The song recounts the torture suffered by a Jewish virgin who would not recant the faith of her fathers in favor of the law of Islam, even under the cruelest constraints. Denounced to the governor by a schemer named Tara, Sol was condemned and then imprisoned. The tribunal warned her: "As a Muslim you will live! As a Jew you will die!" Sol knew that she risked death, but she remained firm in her faith:

> *Yo senyor e nasido ebrea,*
> *I ebrea tengoy ke morir.*

> A Jew I was born,
> And a Jew I will die.

And she prepared herself mentally to take leave of her loved ones, standing up to the executioner:

No kyero ser mora. Sige tu ofisyo infame traidor.

I do not wish to convert to Islam. Perform your duty, you infamous traitor.

The sight of her own blood, flowing from her throat cut with the sword, only confirmed her in her resolution to show posterity how the righteous were to conduct themselves:

Ay de mi! ke de penas padesko. . . . Ke mi istorya se estenda en el mundo. Las donzeyas ke tyenen valor, no se fien en ninguna mora, para verse komo se vyo Sol.

Woe is me! What suffering I must endure. . . . May my story be spread through the world so that brave virgins never trust any Moor and none meets the fate of Sol.[6]

Sol—the one who was not a martyr—found herself granted French nationality, by way of reward, when her son, Denis, won first prize in the general mathematics competition. General de Gaulle applauded the exploit by saying, "We lost the prize in mathematics to a little Turk."

Mathilde and Marguerite

In Salonika as in Constantinople the custom used to be that when a woman had successively lost several children at a young age, she would symbolically sell the next born—say, for six little silver spoons—to another family who thus bought the infant in legal fashion, with or without contract, adopting—*mshtebnia, shtebnet*—a child who was not orphaned. A grandfather who had had only granddaughters could thus "adopt" a grandson in order to be certain that kaddish would be recited at his death.[7]

It is because of this custom that the life of Marguerite Cuenca was saved—but why was the name Mercada ("Sold") or Comprada ("Bought") not given to this *restecada*?—Marguerite, daughter of Mathilde Avigdor, who today, ninety years old, deaf and almost blind, embodies the living memory of the Cuenca family.

Mathilde Avigdor was the sixth of seven children born to Elia Avigdor, my great-great-grandfather on my mother's side. A widower after the death of Lea Cohen, who had given him little Joseph—the same one who was accosted on Good Friday in Tarabya—Elia married a second wife, Oro, his first wife's younger sister, thus avoiding the loss of the dowry of the elder sister. Their daughter Mathilde, the half-sister of Joseph, married Isaac Cuenca, from Salonika. A generation later, the two families were again allied, now on the Gabay side, when Ima married Abba. Isaac Cuenca played the stock market; he lost and hanged himself. Mathilde, many of whose children had died young, nevertheless managed to keep her daughter Marguerite alive.

When her husband died, Mathilde was again pregnant. Before the birth, she named the new son Isaac, instead of Chilibon as tradition would have dictated for posthumous children. The *brit mila* took place in a corner of the house, without ceremony for these *nasidos al kanton*. She entrusted the newborn to her Cuenca brothers-in-law from Salonika, and left, with her eldest daughter Marguerite, to re-join her own family in Istanbul. In order to spare the widow fresh misfortunes—had she forgotten to fast on Yom Kippur, and so drawn down fate against her? did she not know that laughing on the Sabbath assures happiness for all the coming week?—the Adjiman family took over the care of Marguerite. But Mathilde did not have an easy life of it, and had to earn her way as cashier in a wallpaper store on Istliklal Cadessi, one of the principal commercial arteries in the Pera quarter of the city.

Young Isaac, raised by his uncles, married and had three children, but he fell victim to the invasion of German troops in Salonika on 9 April 1941, when the Greeks çooperated with Hitler's troops. Harassment, insults, blows, and service in the forced labor battalions in July 1942 all prepared the Jews for the arrival of Aloïs Brunner and Dieter Wisliceny in February of 1943, the date on which the Nuremberg laws came into force. Wearing the yellow star became obligatory for every Jew over five years of age; Jewish stores and houses were covered with yellow posters, and three ghettos were established.

You, Isaac, were not as clever as Vidal, the father of Edgar Morin, who exploited his "Spanish" nationality (did he not belong to those 316 families who had always retained their nationality?). The puzzled Germans granted Vidal a *salveconducto*, thanks to which he was able to come and go four times during the hostilities. On 15 March, the first train for Auschwitz-Birkenau left Salonika, deporting all the Jews of the Baron de Hirsch ghetto. Which of those nineteen convoys deporting some fifty thousand Salonikans who took this route between March and May 1943 was yours, Isaac?

It is to you, to all of you, that the poem "Siniza i fumo" of Avner Perets is dedicated:

Siniza i fumo
Bolando, kayendo
En un esfuenyo malo
Sin salvasion.
En la guerta kemada
Asentada la fija.
Pasharos pretos
Apretan su korason.
Siniza i fumo
Inchen sus ojos.
No ay kyen ke la desperte
A darle konsolasion.
Por los sielos, ariva
Pasa la luna
Tapando su kara
Kon una nuve—karvon.

Ash and smoke
Flying, falling.
Into a nightmare
Without rescue.
In the parched garden
The girl sits;
Black birds
Tear at her heart.
Ash and smoke
Fill her eyes;
There is no one to wake her,
To comfort her.
In the sky above
The moon passes,
Hiding her face
In a cloud of ash.[8]

By the end of August 1943, Salonika, the "mother of Israel," was completely purified. After World War II there remained only fifteen hundred Jews, of whom five hundred had Spanish nationality.

3

Constantinople

On the European Shore, in the Galatasaray Quarter

Salomon Cuenca, my paternal grandfather, died too young and I never knew him. On a terrace overlooking the Bosphorus, grandfather Salomon—would I have called him *Papu* (grandfather) or *Nono*?—holds a narghile between his knees.

Unlike the biblical Solomon, the incarnation of wisdom and its limits, this grandfather ruled exclusively over his family. Making a sacrifice to exogamy, unlike his brothers, he was also content with a single wife, Rébecca Nahmias. Rébecca, were you that ingenuous lamb in the heart of the family that the Bible shows us, drawing water and welcoming the stranger, who does not hesitate to follow the chosen one to a distant country? Had you grown up in a saintly ancestral family? It would seem that your father, Moïse, a banker, had two wives, Sara, then Régine, who was the first to install a bathroom in your apartment in Varna.

Salomon and Rebecca Cuenca had as children Victoria, Reginika, Jacob—Abba—and little Flora, who died as a child: "a ravishing child with eyes like velvet," remembers Flora from Miami.

> *Tres ermanikas eran,*
> *Blankaz de roz,*
> *I ramas de flor!*

> There were three little sisters,
> White and pink,
> And sprigs of flowers.[1]

The Salomon Cuenca family lived at Toz Koparan Cadessi in two successive apartments, near the Péra Palas Hotel, in the Galata quarter of the city. The summers were spent at Adalar, the Archipelago of the Princes, on one or another of the four islands, Proti, Antigoni, Halki, and Prenkipo, which is the largest. All of them now have Turkish names. In April the whole family moved there for five months: *alevantamos el göç*. They took along the cooler, the mattresses, nothing was to be forgotten! It must have been delicious to take the ferry that crisscrossed the Sea of Marmara to go to the various little towns on the Asiatic coast.

The girls, Régine and Vicky, attended the English High School, and not that of the Alliance Israélite Universelle, which was too common for this "royal" family. They were required to attend one Bible lesson a week: on the Old Testament, which all the pupils attended, but the Jews and the Turks were exempted from the New Testament lesson. *Ke lo bueno!* in that little navy-blue and white uniform, and on their heads, in summer and winter, the white boater with the inscription "English High School." I assume that the school reopened after having been closed when World War I broke out, since Turkey then became the enemy of Britain. Régine's daughter, Rita of San Francisco, wanted to make a pilgrimage there. She brought along the certificate for excellence in history that her mother had been awarded in 1920. Today the school is public and no longer private, but courses are still given in English. Rita was able to visit the entire school, climb the staircase up to the cafeteria, visit all the classrooms, and she is sure that nothing has changed. She met the directress of the school and several teachers and had a great time!

You were born, Abba, in 1908, against the acoustic background of *Hürryet i Vatan, Zito, Zito!* on 14 July, like so many others, if one is to believe the ink-stained registries of the Jewish communities. The issue here was to avoid military service, which had become compulsory for all Ottoman subjects on 23 July 1908, the date of the Young Turks' revolution. Now it included the minorities who until that time had been exempt. It was in 1908 that Haïm Nahoum, supported by the modernizers in the Alliance and favorable to the ideas of the Young Turks, was elected to the position of "acting" chief rabbi, and later, in 1909, to that of chief rabbi for the entire empire.

It was in 1908, too, that the World Zionist Organization opened its first bureau in Istanbul. Very soon, however, in the face of the incessant warring, a pan-Turkish authoritarianism took the place of the liberalism of the Young Turk movement.

For you, Jacob, your parents chose the Brothers of Saint Joseph, in Moda, on the Asiatic shore, a holiday spot for Istanbul residents, with its dance halls and grand hotels. You were a boarder at the school, Abba! You were not happy there, it would seem, especially when you had to recite in chapel "Our Father who art in heaven . . ." instead of *Adonai elohenu*. Were young Muslims similarly obliged? In order to "wash off" the sign of the cross that was made over you each morning, you used to recite to yourself, or so you said, the Shema Israel. Perhaps you relived the story of your distant marrano ancestors Joancho and Isabel: at Kol Nidre on Yom Kippur all the crypto-Jews would cover their faces with their shawls. You learned French because your sisters were learning English. And of course, at home, you spoke only djudyo.

The year 1921: You are thirteen years old, Jacob, an adult male in the religious sense, the age at which marranos revealed to their sons the secret of their descent. For you, there was no secret; you always knew, and one of the first grave recommendations that you made to your daughter Sara was "Never forget!" To meet the requirements of your bar mitzvah, you had to learn by heart, "like a parrot," you said, a passage from the Parashah for the week of your birth: *U-ve-yom hakim et hamishkan*, "on the day the Tabernacle was set up."[2] Hebrew was, in fact, still not the "national" language of the Jews. It would be designated as such only in 1924, after the foundation of the Turkish Republic by Kemal Atatürk. Judeo-Spanish, the language of your ancestor Joancho, was still your language.

Thirteen, time for you Jacob, to complete your education: you had had enough contact with the Greek, Turkish, and Armenian boys in the streets of Galata, and your parents, Rébecca and Salomon, decided that you, Jacob, had nothing more to learn in Istanbul. You had to leave for Vienna. Since the end of the nineteenth century Vienna and Paris had exerted a comparable pull on those interested in study and culture. You already knew French, *djudezmo*, Turkish, Greek, Armenian, and a little English, since Vicky and Reginika were taking classes at the English High School. Did you also know Bulgarian? You used to have fun calling out to your mother-in-law in Russian, *Kak vy pozhivaete, babushka?* A Jew who did not speak several languages was considered feeble-minded at that time. *Ijo mio a la eskola tu te iras, i el tudesko te ambezaras.* Does the world not hang on the breath of children who go to school? Aside from the bankers and distinguished merchants, large numbers of brilliant youths from the East filled the Viennese theaters, where they absorbed the light of Western culture.

In the month of Adar in 1921, little Esther, Rozika, your future wife, although you don't know it yet, is born on the Asiatic shore. Thirteen—it was early in life to be confronting a foreign country all on your own. But no doubt you already knew Vienna; you had uncles living there, and your mother, Rébecca, was a frequent traveler on the Orient Express, seizing the least family occasion, the innumerable bar mitzvahs, engagements, marriages of this huge scattered family, to set out with all her little *michpaha* for the four corners of the Ottoman Empire or of Europe.

You probably didn't know the strange legend about the origin of the Viennese Sephardic community, founded by Moïse Lopez Perera in early 1730. At a time when the Inquisition still ruled in Spain in 1728, a woman approached the main entrance of the Inquisition in Madrid on a stormy night. She sought to obtain from the inquisitor general, Don Diego de Aguilar, clemency for her daughter, condemned to be burned at the stake the next morning at dawn; her only crime was to be a Jewess. In the face of the inquisitor's refusal, the tearful woman cried out:

"Can you not spare her, even if I reveal that this girl is your sister and that this woman on her knees in front of you is none other than your mother?"

And then the poor woman told her own story to the inquisitor general. A few days after her husband had been condemned to the stake and she and her daughter had been authorized to accept the Christian faith, she gave birth to a son. Raised in the Jewish faith, he was kidnapped at the age of seven by the Inquisition, while the mother and sister managed to escape. Several years later, however, they returned to Madrid, where the girl was arrested and condemned to death.

"You were my son, your name was Moses Perera," the woman revealed.

Moved by the discovery of his past, the inquisitor decided to intervene. However, it was too late to save his elder sister. Leaving his monk's habit and wearing a gold chain, the gift of the archduchess Maria-Theresa, the ex-inquisitor left in the company of his mother, who died en route, to solicit the protection of Emperor Charles VI in Vienna. Soon his talents won him the favor of the court and chancellor, so that a number of Jewish families came to Vienna to settle. One day, however, a rumor reached him that the Sephardim would be expelled from Austria. Despite the reassuring words of his friend the chancellor, the empress would no longer receive him. Perera then approached the celebrated Spanish Jew of Constantinople, the prince of Camondo, in the hope of having the sultan intervene. Several weeks later, a special envoy was sent to Vienna and delivered a letter from his sovereign to the empress. Maria-Theresa summoned her council, and after a secret session she notified the sultan that she conceded with pleasure to his request, all the more so since the expulsion of the Jews had never been decided on. The same day, the council was dissolved and the chancellor was charged with appointing a new one. He wanted to call on Perera, but he had left Vienna without anyone knowing his destination; was it Bucharest or Amsterdam?[3]

In Vienna, Jacob, you now lived in a boarding school. Victor Frances, your first cousin, the son of Sarina Cuenca and Bohor Frances, was already established there with his young wife, Djemille Bensasson. Likewise, the youngest of your uncles, David Cuenca, and his niece-*sposika* Flora. Perhaps you lived with them on Ausstellungsstrasse or perhaps with the eldest of your uncles, Joseph. By the time you arrived, your uncle Meier had already left. Nelly, his daughter, remembers witnessing the funeral of the Emperor Franz-Joseph from the heights of the balcony of the Hotel Continental on the Danube, where they lived. In 1904 Tsio Meier had become interested in Zionism. He had met Herzl at the Basel congress, and in Vienna had organized receptions in honor of Jabotinsky, who tried to convince Jews to immigrate to Palestine. Mistaken for a notorious smuggler with the same name, Tsio Meier was imprisoned for thirty-six hours by the Austrian police before being released. The family moved to Budapest, but, alas! one day part of the fortune that Meier always carried with him in his briefcase fell into the water while he was rowing on Lake Balaton! When the communist revolution came, led by Béla Kun, they left again, this time for Lugano. Once again, Meier's cleverness was foiled: he stuffed a slab of butter with jewels and pieces of gold, but the butter was stolen at the Swiss border.

With your uncles in Vienna, as at home in Galata, you spoke Judeo-Spanish and French, Abba. But you had to learn German, the language of business. Even if you had been old enough to attend the lectures of Karl Kraus, who drew a large audience of fervent admirers, you wouldn't have had the idea: you were destined for business, you were the only son, and as such, *ijo regalado*, you were to take over "Cuenca Frères," since your uncles were beginning to get old. Perhaps you used to go to meetings of the Esperanza Society, one of the countless associations with Zionist ideals that, however, had no real political, ethnic, or religious purpose but instead provided recreational gatherings, balls, and other light-hearted festivities. But you certainly celebrated holy days in the synagogue on Cirkus Street, built in the Moorish style of the Alhambra of Grenada.

You were enrolled at the Stubenbastei Realgymnasium. You tried out cigarettes, unless you were just pretending, in the company of your fellow students at the photographer's in order to shock your parents and sisters. On Sunday, a stroll in the Prater Park, where you enjoyed the games of chance, or an outing to the Karwendel Mountains. You always retained a taste for peaks, alpenstocks, rustic leather shorts, and hats with feathers. Later, in another life, you were keen to show me these mountain landscapes, the majestic route of trips back from the Adriatic to Austria, Switzerland, the Black Forest, where our marvelous vacations ended.

On one of her return trips from Vienna to Istanbul for the summer holidays, Rébecca gave a huge party in honor of her prodigal son. Jacob was overwhelmed by the music, dancing, drinking, the joyous atmosphere of his large family. Rébecca asked him reproachfully, "Aren't you worried about your little sister, Florika?" "That's right, where's Florika? Already in bed?" Florika was dead, carried off by one of those childhood illnesses, but the family had not wanted to trouble Jacob's school year with the sad news. Jacob had adored Florika, his youngest sister. He left the party to cry in private, overcome with remorse.

In the days that followed, the comfortable life of Istanbul surrounded him again. Jacob had a good ear, even if he could not read music. He would entertain himself on the family piano by picking out melodies from operettas performed by traveling companies, using two fingers. Then his older sisters, Vicky and Régine, picked up the tunes, all for the greater pleasure of Nono Salomon. The trio of siblings got along wonderfully well; scarcely five years separated them. Life seemed an endless party: a snowy landscape, winter boots, fur collars, toques, Régine and Vicky in a snowball fight. A third girl, in the middle, unknown. "With love from your sisters, March 2nd 28" (in English!). The three of them sunbathing on the rocks of Prenkipo, horseback riding, tennis games, celebrations, trips: a "royal family" indeed! Vicky and Régine again, posing like princesses, with their skirts flared out, huge serious eyes. Postcards without dates. The photographer: Sebah & Joailler, Cons^{ple}. It seemed that no young man in Constantinople dared to ask for their hand in marriage, so inaccessible did they seem.

But Jacob had to leave again. This time it was for Leipzig, where a business school was being established. In Leipzig, there was no family to receive you. It was back to the boarding school, which gave you a lasting taste for discipline. In Leipzig as in Vienna, Jacob filled his spare time with bobsledding and became a champion. Is that why you dreamed that I would win similar prizes? At the age of five I was skiing, at seven you engaged a special instructor to teach me to skate, and at ten you signed me up for tennis. You spared neither your efforts nor your money: your daughter had to have the same life as Reginika and Vicky!

So you learned German. Of the eight languages you knew—didn't you all have a gift for languages?—it was German that you mastered best, without the least trace of accent. The astonishment of your German-speaking interlocutors after the war: your tanned oriental pasha's face just didn't fit in. Your uncle Meier had been representing the Kolbus, Krause, and Fomm companies since 1932. You became the Kolbus representative, and I still remember the Bakelite taste of the olive-green ball-point pens of my childhood that had that brand name. How could you want to work with them again? As for Nelly and Raoul, other cousins, they had become sales representatives for an egg-sorting plant, but Jacky, for his part, wanted to have nothing more to do with Germany. You also decided that I should learn to understand German, on the pretext that it is always better to know the enemy's language. But this language never became alien to you, a mad language; the Germans were never reduced to "Huns" in your eyes, and German, far from being identified with the language of the killers, remained the language in which you passed on to me the poems that you had learned—*Wer reitet so spät durch Nacht und Wind, Es ist der Vater mit seinem Kind,*[4] the language in which you sang to put me to sleep—*Guten Abend, Gute Nacht, mit Rosen bedacht.*[5]

During World War II half of Turkey's commercial dealings were still with Germany. Although there were rumors that Jews were being burned in the baking ovens of Balat, the "Levantine Israelites" still remained "special protégés." What could you, in Turkey, make of the dark times in which Europe was foundering? Were you not afraid for those cousins who had settled of their own free will in France and who suddenly were being hunted on the very soil they had chosen? No doubt you naively believed that their Turkish nationality would protect them, since Turkey was not a party to the conflict. Yet thirteen hundred Jews with Turkish nationality were among those deported from Drancy to Auschwitz. This is what happened to your cousins Marie and Fortunée, Élise's daughters, of whom you never spoke, Abba. They, too, settled in Bayonne, were deported never to return in January 1944.

No doubt the echoes of the suffering reached you well enough: the Frances cousins, fleeing France in January 1943, found refuge in Istanbul with Tsia Elda and Tsio Sam Bensasson, and Rita, your young cousin born in Vienna in 1924, the one whose name no one took the trouble to enter in the family register, finally discovered what the words *family, warmth, love,* and *tenderness* meant. The specificity of antisemitism could not have been apparent to you; at most it was a new kind of anti-Jewish feeling for you. In the face of the recurring persecutions it would be enough, you thought, to escape to a neutral country, to change nationality, change name, in short, to trick them. You yourself chose this path, Abba, when you in turn put down roots in France, when you didn't want to conceive your child elsewhere than "in French territorial waters." For you, France was always the country that in 1791 was the first to grant its Jews emancipation and equality. Of the Vichy that transformed them once again into persecuted pariahs you wanted to know nothing.

After the war, Vicky, who had married a Bulgarian, Meier Vradjali, emigrated from Sofia to Israel with their two children, Rita and Tico. This was in 1949, but Jacob continued to talk of his "sister in Palestine." Régine lived here and there as her first husband moved about: Spain, Latin America, Egypt, France, the United States, until her divorce. Abba, once Nono Salomon was dead, remained alone with Nona Rebecca, his dear mother. Cuenca Frères having gone bankrupt, he had to find a job—to his great shame. But he rapidly moved up through the ranks and found himself director of Ottach Ticaret Türk Sirketi in Ankara. Jacob left Turkey after his marriage to Rozika in 1945, his new wife having insisted on their return to

France. Abba lost a dearly won position. Too bad, he would just have to go to work for Merkado and Vittalutcho Gabay, his in-laws. When Reginka remarried, now to Isaac (Jo) Pappo, they too took up residence in Paris, and this was the occasion for two members of the old trio to get back together. Vicky also came to France regularly. She smoked Winstons and Rozika picked up the habit from her. I still remember Abba's grief when he received news of Reginika's passing in 1970. I had never seen Abba cry before. Then it was Vicky's turn, in 1983; that day, Ima stung Abba with the pitying remark: "Now you're alone in the world."

On the Asiatic Shore

The Gabays, who would become your in-laws and partners, lived on the Asiatic shore. *Gabay* in Hebrew meant treasurer, financier, the administrator of a synagogue. You certainly loved *las paras*, Papu, but I never heard that you, Merkado, or Menahem were descended from these Gabays who, on the model of the Mendes and Carmonas, were the bankers of the janissaries, accumulating colossal fortunes until the dissolution of this corps by Mahmud II in 1826. Neither were you descended from Yehezhiel Gabay, the Baghdad banker, or from Meir Ibn Gabay (1480–1540), the cabalist, critic of Maimonides, and author of the *Avodat Hakodesh* (The Divine Service).

You were born, Papu, in Istanbul in 1881, and you were called Merkado or Menahem ("Marco" in France), the son of a taverner carried off in his youth by tuberculosis and buried in Kadikoy. Each Yom Kippur eve, you would set out with your harem first by ship and then by carriage to go and tidy up your father's grave. Merkado is not a real first name but a substitute for the original name of one who has just escaped a fatal illness, a mortal danger, just like Haïm, Menahem, Vidal, Vita. It is sometimes also given to a male child who replaces an elder brother who died prematurely.

From which peril had you escaped? Which of your older brothers were you supposed to replace? You would, in turn, call your first-born Haïm, after your own father. Haïm became Vittali, a name meaning "life," but why André in French, rather than Henri, as the customary code of transcriptions would have had it? Clearly, there were dangers that you were warding off, precautions against the evil eye, fingers secretly taking the shape of horns! To protect me, my own parents, perhaps on your recommendation, always pinned a little blue stone to the pillow of my childhood bed, in the Turkish fashion.

From you I possessed, without quite knowing how, a passport. You lived in Çiçli, a fashionable neighborhood. You set up house there after a great fire had ravaged the Daghamman suburb where you were then on holiday. From the burning house—*Yangin var! Yangin var!*—you succeeded in rescuing all your little girls, but Mamu begged you to go back in and save the portrait of her young brother Nissim. Although his name was synonymous with "miracle," he died of typhus in 1919. During the Armenian genocide, you sheltered three families that you housed on your seventh floor, where the laundry was usually done using ashes before being spread out on the one of the two patios open to the sky. In the evening, gathered around the *mangal*, you would listen to the moving account of their wild flight across the deserts of Turkey to Constantinople. Among these fugitives was Siranouch, who had lost her husband in the massacres and had also lost track of her two sons. She would find them again, twenty years later, in Marseilles, through the intermediary of the Red Cross.

One day Mamu asked her servant, Fathma, a woman of color: "Why do you seem so sad? I don't want sad people in my house!"

Fathma confessed that she was pregnant. When her time came, Mustapha, our odd jobs man, the one who brought the bundles of washing to the *hamam*, the Turkish bath, was sent to ask for news at the hospital. He came back alarmed. "Her child is white!"

Fathma came back to the house in the company of her baby. He was called Ibrahim, and all the little girls were crazy about him.

Cousin Beky in Jerusalem wrote: "We used to be a large family, but now we are scattered all over. On the Asian shore lived the Gabays. . . . After a great fire, everyone went over to the European side, to Istanbul. It was at that time that Uncle Merkado said that he had to leave for Paris, because of his children, in order to give them a better education. . . . This was in 1925, I think." She was not off by much.

On 11 August 1927—when all your children had already been born—you embarked alone, Papu, "without companions" as the document stated, with "Paris and other foreign countries" as your destination for the purpose of "business." Your description: "Average height, round face, dark complexion, chestnut hair, light eyes"— wait, none of us children had that—"regular nose and mouth, brown mustache, shaven cheeks"—when I knew you, you had a beard. Your trip lasted three months: after Paris, there was Italy, Switzerland, Bulgaria, Russia. I owned a pretty leather suitcase all covered with customs stickers that was yours and that Ima gave me at your death. But where is it now?

Crisscrossing Europe, you seem to have been looking for the best place to settle with your family. Since 1924 all Jewish schools in the Ottoman Empire had been subject to an official program that considerably diminished the importance of French, and they had the choice of teaching either in Turkish or in their supposed maternal language, Hebrew, which few of them used. Perhaps you had a presentiment of the campaign of harassment against those who dared to speak foreign languages in public, and the prohibition of all religious instruction in the schools, that began in the 1930s. You wanted to rejoin your eldest son, who was a boarder at the Michelet secondary school in Vanves, and whom you had sent to France, wishing to spare him from the notorious Turkish military service. You gave up your position as agent for fabrics imported from Manchester. You cleverly moved your fortune abroad, and you soon became an expert in rubber, creating the Mundia company at 5 rue Saulnier. On stationery from the company, your wife, Eléonore Gabay, née Avigdor, wrote these undated lines, in a spelling that is rather phonetic, to her brother Elia, Liatchouna, who had emigrated to Peru to avoid conscription:

Mi kerido ermano Elia,
    Vingo de recivir una karta d'invitation: me diché kyen sea esté Italiano ke se yama Elia Avigdor Cohen. Despoues me pinsi pouédesser ke es el

ijo de mi ermano. Ya pensas mi allegria de imaginarmé ke es Jojo ke té esta dando esta contantés à la végés. Boueno ke passé amen i té allegrés. Siempré tingo saloudés touyos ke mé mandas por Albert. Ya esta bueno agora. Touvo oun accidenté ke sé kayo i eskapo de la mouerte. Estouvo 15 dias al hopital. Agora ya esta boueno kon esto. Souetto boueno ke passé amen. Te ambrasso por toda la familla. Tou kérida ermana ke te ambrassé.
    Eléonore Gabay.

Mi kérido Jojo touvé grande allégria ke te estas casando i ke sé allégré Papa in sou végés. Bueno ke passés kon tou quérida mouger i in ora bouena ke séa. Embrassas a Clairette por mi.

My dear brother Elia,

    I have just received an invitation card and I asked myself: who is this Italian who calls himself Elia Avigdor Cohen? Then I thought, perhaps it's my brother's son! Imagine how happy I was at the idea that it is Jojo who is giving you so much pleasure in your old age. May everything go well, amen to that, and may you be happy. Albert asks me to say hello. He is well at the moment. He had an accident and fell and just escaped death. He spent fifteen days in the hospital. I send you kisses from all the family. Your dear sister, who embraces you.
    Eléonore Gabay.

My dear Jojo, it gave me great pleasure to learn that you are getting married and to imagine your father's joy in his old age. May this union with your dear wife take place under a good sign, and give Clairette a kiss from me.

Yako, Vida, Salomon, Rébecca, Joseph, Rika, David, Meier, Esther, Sarina, Élise, Fortuna, Vicky, Régine, Flora, Jacob: the beautiful names of my Cuenca family delighted me. I even took pleasure in repeating over and over again those of the maternal branch: Merkado, Léa, Oro, Estréa, Rachel, Elia, Nissim, Vittali, Sultana, Luna, Klara, Esther.

Turkey—I imagined the sounds, colors, smells, bits of my parents' childhood: the cries of street merchants, the baskets that were lowered from the balconies of houses of black wood, the *yalis*, and that were hauled up filled with food. The beaker of fresh water from the water carrier. The bathtub of my mother, the last-born and most spoiled, that you put on the balcony to warm up in the sun. Sundays at Burgaz or Büyük Ada: the row of little girls in their starched dresses, fresh from the hamam—*Ya sale Melisenda de los banyos de banyar*[6]—who, with their picnic baskets full of *borekitas, halva, kaymak, hummus,* and *kefte,* were waiting for the little steamboat. At times, on holiday on the Adriatic coast, my parents would evoke *kon eskarinyo* the odor of the roses of Istanbul—I believe that the roses came from Isfahan—the call of the muezzin: *La illah il allah.*

From this grandfather, at least, I have many more memories, since he and practically all his family settled in France in 1931. But these are memories of France.

A photo taken on rue Léon-Bonnat, the year of my birth: you are wearing a beret, holding a wriggling doll in your delighted grandfatherly arms, the offspring of your youngest daughter, your favorite, the prettiest, the last-born, but doubtless also the most obedient, she who never dared to rebel against your law, the one who disappointed you least. But I would soon be displaced, dethroned. Judith, four years younger than I, the daughter of your eldest son, would steal your heart from me. In the normal course of things she would be brought up in the Jewish faith, would eat kosher food, would learn Hebrew, would have her bat mitzvah. She lived in the apartment building next to yours, and it would be she who took her piano lessons in your sitting room with its chairs and sofas always in slipcovers and smelling of mothballs, where the bier would be set up—why in the sitting room?—and we would contemplate the mask of Mamu. "Isn't she beautiful?" Tsia Sultana whispered to me, already busy sorting through the lace, on her knees in front of the clothes chests, the keys to which Mamu, as mistress of the house, always jealously carried at her waist. The rabbi, the one from rue Copernic—well, I didn't know until then that you had gone over to the liberals of the 16th arrondissement!—murmured prayers while rocking in a corner. This was my first contact with death, my first burial, and I didn't understand why I was being served hard-boiled eggs, olives, and dates. It was to give me courage to face what was to follow. Soon the hearse arrived. Vittali insisted that Rozika, as the youngest daughter, accompany him, the eldest son, in the hearse. Ima had a hysterical out-burst, cried, argued, and called Abba for help. Abba was devastated and a bit of a coward. He was content to say, "We shouldn't have let Rozika get in, she is too delicate," and he wiped away a tiny tear of remorse.

One day, Ima and Abba left on a few days' trip to London to patch up marital differences. I was left in the apartment on rue Poussin with Éva, our maid at the time, but Éva took me every day for *merenda* at my grandparents'. On rue Léon-Bonnat I would stick my pudgy hand into the wooden candy jar carved with little flowers, but not before having inhaled the intense aroma of bergamot of the candy from Haci Bekir's pastryshop, one of the most famous in Is-tanbul, that impregnated the lid. *Kyeres un bonbon, hanum, hanumika?* No one would ever address me in that way again. *No yores, mi alma.* At your place, Abba, the candy jar was from Chez Christofle and was always filled with stuffed dates, almonds, Turkish delights. You and Ima used to reach into it from either side of the table while watching television. Papu chased Mamu around the table, threatening her with his cane; she evaded him uttering the cries of a wounded bird. You are still capable of arguing! Éva quickly brings me home to rue Poussin. But we are at my grandparents' again the day my parents come home. I unwrap the present that they have brought me, a huge doll of milky wax with wonderfully curly, black hair, dressed in navy-blue gabardine; it could walk when you took its hand. I don't remem-ber what name I gave it; in any case I would change it each week, giv-ing me the chance to rebaptize it in the garden of my friends, the little Popesco girls.

It is Sunday, and as usual we have come to pay you a visit. Today there are *malebis* with a taste of rosewater and cinnamon. Abba is out of breath and beside himself. He has just spent hours on the allées of Saint-Cloud Park holding me by my sweater so that I would finally learn to ride my bike without training wheels. You lived on the ground floor and both of you used to read in front of the window, facing each other in leather armchairs that had been scratched by the cats. You, Papu, always had your prayer book in your hand and you rocked tirelessly. Mamu, she had had an account for years with the Lavocat bookstore on avenue Mozart, and the bookseller would tear her hair every time Ima went there to get her new books. You had already read and reread everything they had in stock according to their card index, and one can't give too modern a novel to an elderly woman of your age and education. But did you really read or was it enough just to keep your eyes occupied? The people of the Book! We had to knock on the windowpane to inform you of our arrival, for you had both become a bit deaf and we got upset when you still hadn't picked up the telephone after the fifth ring. We had to come to make sure nothing had happened to you, and you refused to give us a key. You had difficulty walking as well. To spare you the trouble of going to the bathroom at the end of a long, dark corridor, since you would not turn the light on—it wasn't the Sabbath, just the Gabay stinginess—we installed for you, Papu, a urinal in the kitchen pantry, which was closer. I didn't dare to go near the kitchen after that. Mamu would come, shuffling in her slippers: *Ke haber, kerida?* But it's you, Papu, to whom I wanted to show my accomplishments of the day. But I had to be patient, had to sacrifice to ritual. No, today I will not kiss your hand; it's not a holy day. For once, you pretend to be understanding: you pinch my cheek between your two fingers that you then bring to your lips, but you pinch too hard, just to make me feel your dissatisfaction. Now my cheek is red. In order to punish me for my insolence, you play a trick. You let your *kipa* slip from your smooth, bald skull on purpose, and you throw me a glance that clearly says: pick it up for me. I have to comply, put it back in place. I don't like the stuffy smell of that kipa. Finally, you come up to the window, dressed as always in your Scottish dressing gown, and you admire, with eyes faded by cataracts, your granddaughter who shows off her bike-riding in the street. Behind the wall of the dead end is the Auteuil Orphanage, where I often go with Ima to see the Sissi films on rainy Sundays. I don't yet know what *orphan* means.

You used to come, but very rarely, to rue Molitor to visit your youngest daughter. Ima was finally furnishing her own place. Until now she had always lived, to her great shame, in furnished apartments. Now, she was going to antique stores. She had just bought a carved wooden bishop, which she boldly perched on a butcher's block in the hallway. You were furious: what was that saint doing in her house? You threw your hat over it to cover it up.

It is Yom Kippur. Despite your advanced age, you have fasted all day, spent the whole day in prayers at the ENIO, on rue Michel-Ange, which is still run by the man who would later become my philosophy teacher. When evening comes, we join you. I don't understand anything, but I am moved and I adore the sound of the *shofar*. I have the feeling of belonging to a huge family. Was it you who advised my parents to enroll me in classes in religious instruction and Hebrew? I didn't stay there very long, preferring the courses in home economics. In particular, I learned how to make almond cakes. Although they are not very oriental, you appreciated these pastries very much and I often brought you some: *Benditchas las manos ke tal fizyeron!* you would exclaim. We leave the temple to go your place. I keep an eye out for the first star in the sky, which will authorize me to throw myself over the delicacies that Mamu has been preparing for more than a week. First, you have to line your stomach: little bits of bread are dunked in a bowl of spiced oil, and you drink a cup of coffee with milk. People are chatting away and it's very noisy. Sultana finds a way to ask Abba in a falsely pleading tone whether he will be able to pay her her allowance this month too. Why doesn't she ask her father, her brother? She is sure that they will refuse, but Abba, he never says no, and throughout his life he would send small sums to support his widowed sisters, "so that they won't want for anything," which puts Ima beside herself and which my maternal aunts make so much fun of. His whole life, Abba would be exploited, by his mother, by his sisters, by Ima . . .

The room seems beautiful, beaming with light, but the Pesach ritual was even more mysterious. Why didn't we go throw our sins into the Seine, as the devout Jews of Bulgaria did into the Danube?[7] Unless that was on Rosh Hashanah. As for children, there are only Sara, Judith, and Marco, Vittali's children; those of Luna and the "white Russian" had been baptized during the war. Is that why you refuse them a place at your table? We parade past you, the youngest first, to kiss your hand and receive your blessing in return, your hand flat on our heads, you chant, *Yo te bendigo* . . . Amen!

August 1960. We are on holiday on the Adriatic coast, as was often the case, Abba not wishing at any price to set foot again in Spain before the death of Franco—wait! once we did go to Majorca, to the Chuetas. Did you not know, Abba, that on 20 December 1924, during the dictatorship of Primo de Rivera, the Sephardim were invited to apply for the nationality of their ancestors, including former "protected" residents and their descendants, before 31 December 1930. For all that, granting nationality was not the same thing, it's true, as granting the right of return and resettlement: "The race of Jacob is everywhere an element that is pernicious to the sound mentalities of Westerners," argued Duque de Amalfi, the diplomatic agent of Spain in Bucharest.[8]

Ima has received a telegram. You have passed on to the "world of truth," Papu, you will no longer ritually rock over your prayers, you will say your amber beads no more, I will no longer bake *pastelikos* for you. Rozika seems overcome. Never again will she bow humbly over your thin hand, *Le bezo las manos, senyor padre*. I was left in Italy without my views being solicited, alone on the beach, under the tent. Alone in the dining room where the other guests took pity on me and passed along the news: *è morto il nonno*. The *avvocato*, whose corset I saw drying every day on the wires of the *bagnini* Virgilio and Virgilia, takes advantage of the circumstances to take me out one evening to eat *gelato al limone*. When they come back, Ima was very silent and often pushed me away. *Dechala*, Abba ordered me, forgetting that our private language was French, and he said to Rozika: *no te merekyes, hanum*—but wait! I thought that gentle word was reserved for me! Abba too is more serious, more attentive. No doubt he loved his father-in-law a bit; he had lost his own father very young—"my dear father!" he would say, followed by a great sigh. Did Makhlouf and Marco attend the ceremony? And the white Russian, Tsio Michel? There are few men in this family; it would always be difficult to assemble the *minyan*. Tsio Vittali recited kaddish, in his capacity of oldest—and only—son.

You would never again crumble your bread into your soup, you would never again lay claim to *el trontcho* of the salad. Would I ever eat *laban* with cinnamon again? Now that you are no longer here, who will do the shopping at the Eradjian Brothers? As a souvenir of you, I asked for your prayer book. Well, you hadn't read to the end of it, and you needed a bilingual French-Hebrew edition! Much later Klara gave me your Book of Psalms. On page 10, Psalm 18, the one that begins with the verse "I love you, O Lord, my strength," I found serving as a page marker the childish drawing of a lemon by your grandson Marco as well as a Social Security payment for 288 old francs, dated 29 December 1959. Ima, she gave me your cane.

The last photograph of you: in Flins, at your son's country house; you must have been proud that he had put down roots. Abba, no doubt jealous, would say: "My brother-in-law has a unique view of the Renault factory!" Likewise, Tsia Klara would buy a house near Houdan, *maşallah, esto i muntcho*, where Mamu would often go after your death. This house would also be the scene of my adolescent loves.

In order to replace you with Mamu, who had at least gained the advantage of no longer being tyrannized, who no longer had to rush in, Turkish slippers in one hand, coffeepot in the other, to answer your imperious ring of the bell, no more parsley omelets to be hastily prepared when your stomach felt a little empty. "Tenants" were found to occupy that sad apartment and look after her a bit. But one of them had knocked her down, the poor old woman! She recovered—touch wood!—but she aged more and more. Ima and Luna go once a month to give her *un buen banyo*, but the two of them are not strong enough to lift that great mass of flesh—six pregnancies, just half the twelve tribes of Israel!—into the hip bath, scrub her, rub her with *rasoul* clay as she demanded, dye her hair mauve, dry her, and put her to bed. *Ay de mana! Maneate, pateja!* Then, despite her protests, they busy themselves with repairing the disorder of the cupboards filled to bursting with little brown bags from the fruit shop. What was it you used to keep in them? The remains of candles burned on the Sabbath, fruit paste, pistachios, odd stockings, sugar cubes pinched from cafes. Then they bring you your evening meal, a Heudebert biscuit—make sure you don't get the wrong brand or you'd have to take them back!—and your *tchay*: you liked it very strong with a lot of sugar, apple-scented, as in Istanbul, except that there was no samovar, but you still made your own Turkish coffee in a horrible little blue pot. Then they leave you to sleep your short night, worn out, overcome by having become the mother of their mother: *Buenas notches, mana* . . .

It seems that Mamu, Léa-Eléonore-Losi (once again the trail is hard to follow, why not Lia?) Avigdor, your fiancée, had waited seven years for you, Papu, not that you would have preferred a Rachel, the "lady from downstairs" to her, but this was the time you needed to marry off all your younger brothers and sisters, Rachel, Nissim, Maurice, Victoria, as you had made it your duty on the death of your own father. Léa—is it true that this name means "wild cow"?—like many of the women of her generation, was content to be a wife and mother, even if she was not blessed with many sons. As in the Bible, she was the *Akeret habayit*, but I do not think that she was, as in the Bible, the most unfortunate of matriarchs. It is true that you were not Jacob and, if you had four wives, we didn't know anything about it, Papu. On your death, Mamu developed new habits: Saturdays she would go by taxi to her eldest daughter, Sultana, and would sit quietly in a corner of the shop, amused by the comings and goings of customers. Sundays, she would visit us. I would go and pick her up in the car—*la araba de la tchika*! She was always delighted to see how much I had grown. After the Sunday meal, Ima would hole up in her room and try to compensate for her insomnia, escaping the infernal din of "Sunday Sports," and wouldn't come out unless Sultana came to join us for la merenda. Thus Abba remained alone with his mother-in-law. They didn't really have anything to say to each other, even though he always remained respectful. Mamu would spend a few days of vacation in the country, at her daughter Klara's. On her death, I asked Klara, who had found a way to sell everything down to my beloved candy jar, for her portrait in pastels. It had been done by the now deceased husband of Klara, the one who died as a newlywed from a brain tumor. And from this time on it was at the home of your son, Haïm, Vittali, born in Istanbul on 30 January 1911, naturalized by decree on 3 August 1951, that family celebrations were held.

III

BETWEEN EAST AND WEST:
A TIME FOR ALLIANCES

Tres hermanas son.
Las dos eran kazadas,
La una se desperdio.

There were three sisters,
Two were married,
The other was lost.
   —"Las tres ermanikas," Judeo-Spanish song

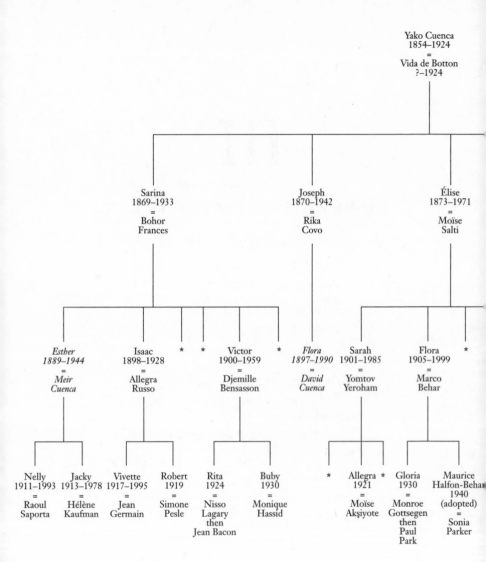

Yako Cuenca
1854–1924
=
Vida de Botton
?–1924

Sarina
1869–1933
=
Bohor
Frances

Joseph
1870–1942
=
Rika
Covo

Élise
1873–1971
=
Moïse
Salti

Esther
1889–1944
=
Meir
Cuenca

Isaac
1898–1928
=
Allegra
Russo

*   *

Victor
1900–1959
=
Djemille
Bensasson

*

Flora
1897–1990
=
David
Cuenca

Sarah
1901–1985
=
Yomtov
Yeroham

Flora
1905–1999
=
Marco
Behar

*

Nelly
1911–1993
=
Raoul
Saporta

Jacky
1913–1978
=
Hélène
Kaufman

Vivette
1917–1995
=
Jean
Germain

Robert
1919
=
Simone
Pesle

Rita
1924
=
Nisso
Lagary
then
Jean Bacon

Buby
1930
=
Monique
Hassid

*

Allegra
1921
=
Moïse
Akşiyote

*

Gloria
1930
=
Monroe
Gottsegen
then
Paul
Park

Maurice
Halfon-Behar
1940
(adopted)
=
Sonia
Parker

The Cuenca *michpaha*

Only those persons mentioned in one way or another in the text are listed here by name.
Others are represented by an asterisk (*). The descendants of Meier and Esther, like those of
David and Flora (in italics), have been listed only once.

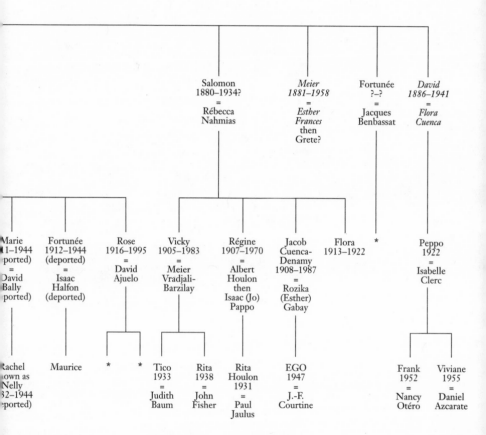

Salomon
1880–1934?
=
Rébecca
Nahmias

Meier
1881–1958
=
Esther
Frances
then
Grete?

Fortunée
?–?
=
Jacques
Benbassat

David
1886–1941
=
Flora
Cuenca

Marie
1–1944
ported)
=
David
Bally
ported)

Fortunée
1912–1944
(deported)
=
Isaac
Halfon
(deported)

Rose
1916–1995
=
David
Ajuelo

Vicky
1905–1983
=
Meier
Vradjali-
Barzilay

Régine
1907–1970
=
Albert
Houlon
then
Isaac (Jo)
Pappo

Jacob
Cuenca-
Denamy
1908–1987
=
Rozika
(Esther)
Gabay

Flora
1913–1922

*

Peppo
1922
=
Isabelle
Clerc

Rachel
own as
Nelly
32–1944
ported)

Maurice

*

*

Tico
1933
=
Judith
Baum

Rita
1938
=
John
Fisher

Rita
Houlon
1931
=
Paul
Jaulus

EGO
1947
=
J.-F.
Courtine

Frank
1952
=
Nancy
Otéro

Viviane
1955
=
Daniel
Azcarate

I

The Cuenca Michpaha

Your sister Régine was born 15 April 1907; she was just fourteen months older than you, Abba. She celebrated her first marriage on 21 October 1930 with Albert Houlon, who was originally from Turkey. Their daughter, Rita of San Francisco, heard it said, without being really sure, that her grandfather Houlon was the concierge in Nono Salomon Cuenca's building. In any case, young Albert, after having seen the photo of Tsia Régine at the home of common friends, fell in love with her and asked for her hand in marriage. Rébecca and Salomon were all the more pleased as Albert didn't want a dowry, his fiancée's beauty being enough for him. Thus, the single dowry of the family could go, as was proper, to the eldest daughter, Vicky, who—and here tradition was not served—was not yet married. The dowry was something that had to be started at birth:

embroidering and monogramming every blouse, every sheet, every housecoat. Accumulate furs, furniture, household linen, Turkish books that would show in the eyes of all of what *buena famiya* the young woman was. If the young man were without employment, an even more substantial dowry would be necessary. If he were well-off, the dowry should be no less considerable, for he had to be compensated for taking on the financial burden of a wife! From all this came the anguish and hysterical tears of young mothers giving birth to several daughters: *la ninya en la facha, el achugar en la kacha!*

Their marriage was celebrated in Paris, and Albert posed for a photograph in the bois de Boulogne on 26 October 1930 in the company of Régine, who looks like a princess draped in furs. Then a honeymoon to Madrid: a somewhat affected and well-behaved schoolgirl in front of the Neptune fountain—"Riginetta, 9 November." Or, devastatingly Sephardic, hands on her hips, in front of the Museum of Modern Art a week later. Radiant, in panne velvet, at the Retiro Park: "Yours, Riggy, 14 December 1930." From the hotel Principe de Asturias, you sent hugs and kisses to your family in January 1931. In a silk negligee, feathered slippers on your feet, holding a book in your hand whose title can't be made out, you looked like Claudette Colbert, and this time, on 3 April 1931, you signed "Ginetta." Had the honeymoon lasted this long or had you settled in Madrid? Again, cloaked in a sumptuous mantilla, your husband straight as a cane hung on your arm: "A souvenir from la Castellena . . . and her husband."

You are pregnant, no one knows it yet, perhaps you were obeying the old superstition not to announce the event before the fifth month. Shortly thereafter, your husband asked you where you wanted to have the baby: Turkey, Egypt, where you then were, or Paris? You chose Paris, and Rita was born there on 30 August 1931. This was not a happy marriage; I remember Abba's awkwardness when I asked him the name of the elegant young man in the photograph with the smiling Régine. "A thwarted love," you sighed.

Régine strikes an even more elegant pose: on a Paris balcony, "Rita at eight weeks." *Ke lo bueno!* Rébecca and Salomon must have sighed from a distance. They did not wait long before taking a trip, as the photos taken in the bois de Boulogne prove. Abba was there too; he

Yako Cuenca and Vida de Botton, Varna, Bulgaria, around 1920. SCD Archives.

Klara (Cohen) and Joseph Avigdor as newlyweds, Constantinople, 1880. SCD Archives.

*Hermine, Leon, and Rozy Policar with their employee in front of their store,
24 rue Dufour, Paris, 1932. J. Policar Archives, Paris.*

Salomon Cuenca and Rébecca (Nahmias) with their children, Plovdiv, Bulgaria, 1913. SCD Archives.

Salomon Cuenca in Bursa (1906). Buby Frances Archives.

Joseph Cuenca and Rika (Covo) in Salonikan costumes, about 1912.

David Cuenca in Vienna, about 1920. Jo Cuenca Archives, Colombia.

Marco Gabay and Eleonore (Avigdor) with their children. Left to right: Klara, Vittali, Sultana, Luna, Esther (Rozika), Constaninople, 1927. SCD Archives.

Jacky Cuenca, about 1920. Rita Frances Archives.

Nelly Cuenca, about 1920. Rita Frances Archives.

Flora Cuenca in Bulgarian peasant dress, about 1910. Jo Cuenca Archives.

In Constantinople about 1925. Back row, right to left: Regine Cuenca, Hermine Policar,
Vicky Cuenca. SCD Archives.

The store of Yüsûk Kalderim in Constantinople, 1925. Right to left: Elia, Becky and Moïse Kohen, with Isaac, the employee. Becky Roza Archives, Jerusalem.

Moïse Nahmias in Varna, Bulgaria, date unknown. SCD Archives.

Luna and Rozika Gabay, Paris, 1938. SCD Archives.

The Salomon Cuenca family. Right to left: Salomon, Rébecca, Vicky, Hermine and Rozy Policar, Regine, Constantinople, about 1925. SCD Archives.

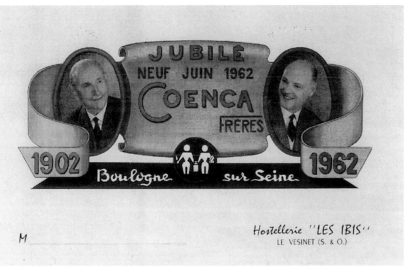

Meier Cuenca and his son Jacky, Paris, 1962. Jo Cuenca Archives.

*Back row, second from
left: Jacob Cuenca, at
the Aşkale camp, Ana-
tolia, Turkey, 1943.
SCD Archives.*

*ID card from the Paris
Prefecture of Police.*

*Rozika Gabay and
Makhlouf, Istanbul,
1 July 1944.
SCD Archives.*

gives the impression of being colossally bored in his new role of uncle. As a "lady in the bois de Boulogne," still looking the princess, you are pushing your baby carriage in October of 1931. The album continues: March 1932, "A warm souvenir from the little family." August 1932, in Paris, still on a balcony, Reggy is disguised as a nursemaid with her little doll standing on a pedestal table. July 1933, "Affectionate kisses from the beach": the Normandy coast, little striped tents. April 1934: "Affectionate souvenirs to Mama and Papa" from Paris.

Then no trace of you until May 1936, in New York, where you arrived in 1935 by ship, once Albert, who had been rewarded with American citizenship for voluntarily enlisting in the American army during World War I, had found a refuge for you. August 1939, the Houlon family at West Point. July 1941, Régine, radiant again, in front of skyscrapers. Your daughter does not look like you, despite your insistence on the two of you dressing as twins! July 1944, Rye Beach, Albert Houlon, Mrs. Bensignor, Zelda Avigdor, Régine, Jacques Avigdor, Mr. Bensignor, and their daughter. 12 February 1945, in English: "To mother & Jacques with love." Régine and Albert divorced in 1954, and she married Isaac Pappo.

Isaac Pappo was the youngest son of Victoria Nahmias, the half-sister of Nona Rébecca, who had come, as the widow of Haïm Pappo, to Paris in the 1920s in the company of her six sons. Haïm was a prominent member of the Jewish community of Haskovo, having dandled the son of the king of Bulgaria on his knee. He owned an oil well in Romania. He was imprisoned with two of his sons, Salomon and Moïse, in Ploieşti, because all three of them were Bulgarians and thus the enemies of the regime. Once demobilized after the war of 1914–18 they left for Russia to set up an import-export business. Haïm was again arrested and died in prison. Victoria, who had joined him there, was freed. Salomon, Simantov, Jacob, Albert, Moïse, Isaac: what did you live on? Salomon Pappo, the eldest brother, and his wife Berthe Pardo lived on rue de la Gaîté. This is probably why my childhood memory has retained the impression of such a welcoming household! Later I learned that Salomon had been a senior officer in the Masonic movement. Was this a way of not standing out as a Jew, a vestige of marranism, or was it a true affiliation with the universalist ideals of freemasonry? In the family album I found a photograph of Salomon and Berthe Pappo at Luna Park in the company of their cousins Léon and Hermine Policar, arrivals from Plovdiv, the former Philippopolis, which had become Turkish in 1390 and then Bulgarian in 1885. Hermine and Léon tried their luck with a clothing store on rue du Four under the name "Janie-Rose." Business was bad, they left again for Bulgaria, leaving behind their son Jacques who was a student at the faculty of dentistry and who, to top up his monthly allowance, worked as a photographer in the nightclubs on the Champs-Élysées. Jacques enlisted in the army in 1939, at the age of twenty. After France's armistice with Germany, he fled Paris and from Bordeaux tried to make his way to England. Turned back, he tried his luck at Port-Vendres. Alas! the ship on which he had clandestinely taken passage put him ashore in Oran. From there Jacques left for Casablanca, where he settled until 1950, since Morocco was then a French protectorate.

I had known Régine's second husband well. Isaac—Jo in France—was a doctor on avenue Ledru-Rollin, where I used to recite poetry on Sundays, hidden behind the green plush drapes: *bravo cherika mia!* He was a first cousin of Tsia Régine—we're back to endogamy. Later, Jo told me of his wartime experiences. Taken prisoner by the Germans, he was sent to North Africa to work as a physician. One day, a plane landed in that place blessed by the gods, and on board was an important Nazi functionary and his daughter, a prey to acute appendicitis. As a Jew, Jo was not supposed to touch an Aryan; yet he operated on her. The little girl recovered so quickly that the official offered to have Jo repatriated. But he turned the offer down, convinced as he was that if he came back to Paris he would be arrested again and sent God knows where. Instead, he asked only that he be sent food, medication, and blankets for his troops. Jo then stayed in North Africa until the end of the war. Simantov, another of the Pappo brothers, remained hidden by a Frenchwoman for the duration of the war. Despite his auspicious first name, Besimantov, he would never recover from his tuberculosis.

Vicky, the eldest of you siblings, was born on 21 August 1905. The Cuenca dowry, as we have seen, fell to Uncle Meier, a Bulgarian, met through the intermediary of a *shiduch*. He married her in 1932 and she was thenceforth called Victoria Vradjali. You lived in Sofia, where your two children were born: Tico on 9 March 1933, a bad year, he used to joke, and Rita on 6 February 1938, hardly a better one! Tsio Meier—another uncle that I never knew!—studied engineering in Vienna and later, when the Jews were driven out, in Prague. But he never practiced his profession for all that. Before the war, he worked in the textile industry and, after the war, the communist government gave him a position as an accountant.

According to their daughter, New York Rita—all the girls of this branch of the family bore the name of their paternal great-grandmother, not that of their grandmother—the family lived in a very attractive neighborhood of Sofia, 55 Czar Simeon Street, and not in the Jewish quarter, Baviera, which was the Ashkenazic neighborhood. Along with Serbia, Bulgaria was then an important center for Sephardic Jewry. In 1934 fifty thousand Jews lived there, making up 0.8 percent of the population; half of them lived in Sofia. The great majority of them were Judeo-Spanish speakers, but as for you, you spoke Bulgarian at home. Although he had not been an ardent patriot during World War I, Meier nonetheless integrated, to the point of insisting that you give up our ancestral tongue. He clearly did not understand that in relegating his language to the storeroom it was a bit of his homeland, a bit of his culture, that he was losing. There were, however, some fifty magazines in Judeo-Spanish and in Bulgarian, and literary life in the city was in full flower at the beginning of the century.

Until the nineteenth century, the Jews of Bulgaria were well integrated, on both the social and cultural levels. The Berlin Congress of 1878, at which a treaty was signed after the Russo-Turkish War sealing the creation of the Bulgarian national state, required the Balkan countries to grant civil rights to their minorities. In 1893–94 the first antisemitic periodicals began to appear: *Bulgaria for the Bulgarians*, which by its second issue had become *Bulgaria without Jews*, as well as *Narodna Svoboda* (National Liberty), published by Nikola Mitakov. In 1911 the parliament had no Jewish member to represent the community, a clear sign of the Jews' lack of interest in political life. From 1930 on, with the arrival of the various Fascist movements, things truly began to deteriorate, the ultranationalists engaging in anti-Jewish propaganda that took up the traditional accusations of ritual murder and poisoning. The wealth of some of you was attributed to dishonesty, and discriminatory measures were soon introduced. Jews no longer had the right, for example, to have more than five vehicles in a wedding cortege.

But you didn't seem too upset as yet, and the family album still has a lighthearted air: Vicky and Tico, March 1936, "For Grandma and Uncle Jacob, a souvenir from Rita, Sofia, 28 June 1938." Nono Salomon must have died between 1934 and 1938, since he is no longer named in dedications. "Vicky and Rita, March 1940": you are still smiling, although a bill for the protection of the Bulgarian nation, on the model of the Nuremberg laws, had just been drafted. Sofia: "For Grandma, a souvenir from RTV, July 1941." 1941: Bulgaria is now an ally of Germany, and authorizes the passage of troops to Greece and Yugoslavia in April. Vicky, Tico, Rita—Sofia, May 1942. August 1942. A commissariat for Jewish affairs is set up. December 1942: Tsio Meier is still eating out, in restaurants, to the sound of balalaikas.

January 1943: Victor Frances, his wife Djemille, and their daughter Rita, fleeing France for Istanbul, stop over with you. Since the middle of 1942 Bulgarian Jews have been wearing the yellow star—*limpieza de sangre*. A distinctive sign—on the model of the *señal real?*—is put up on their houses, they are no longer welcome in certain public places, and the men are sent off in special labor gangs on the basis of a law promulgated in "defense of the nation" in November 1940, after the meeting between Boris III with Hitler. On 20 January 1943, at precisely 9:14 P.M., Hauptsturmführer Dannecker, a specialist in Jewish matters, arrived in Sofia. Despite the report that Beckerle sent to Berlin two days later— "Not all the Jews of Bulgaria are rich; some are craftsmen, others workers. Raised in the midst of Greeks, Armenians, Gypsies, and Turks, the average Bulgarian does not grasp the significance of the struggle against the Jews since he is not very concerned with racial problems"[1]—the crucial agreement for the deportation of a first contingent of twenty thousand Jews from the south of Thrace and from Macedonia to eastern Germany was officially signed on 22 February 1943, by Belev and Dannecker.

Sofia, 24 February 1943: it is raining and cold. On 2 March the council of ministers fixed its seal on the fatal document, while deciding not to make a public event of it. The plan of the fanatical Belev foresaw the deportation of all the Jews from Sofia shortly after this first contingent of twenty thousand persons—secrecy, in fact, being essential to counter any mass movement of the Jews who had gone underground. Nevertheless, rumors of the deportation of Jews were spreading. At the end of February, Chayim Bechar, a Jew from Kyustendil visiting Sofia, met Dr. Vater, a venal individual who offered to sell him information. At almost the same time, Belev's personal secretary, Lilyana Panitsa, warned Buko Levi, a member of the official consistory, that he and his wife were on the list of 2,500 persons to be deported from Sofia.[2] Political figures then intervened with Boris III. On 10 March, Archbishop Kiril of Plovdiv sent a telegram to the king, threatening to lie down across the railroad tracks if the deportation plans were realized. Petko Stainkov, Stilyan Chilingirov, and the church synod added their protests. On 21 May, however, a decree by the council of ministers stipulated the expulsion of all Jews from Sofia, sending them first to the countryside, then to death camps outside the country. Three days later, the regional committee of the Bulgarian Communist Party published a tract calling for resistance. A group of communist protesters, Jewish in inspiration, made its way toward the palace. Four hundred persons were arrested and sent to the concentration camp near Somovit.[3]

Ruse, also known as Rustchuk, that city on the Danube where numerous Jews had taken refuge in 1788 when the Austrians attacked Belgrade—Ruse, on the border between Romania and Bulgaria, would be the destination imposed on the Vradjalis. In less than twenty-four hours, you had to pack your bags and find new lodgings. Dommolé, an alias of Nissim Aftalion, the name of your new landlord, puts a protective arm around Rita's shoulder on 18 September 1944. You've become a bit skinny, my little cousin! Tsio Meier works in the camp but comes home every evening. Life was very hard, you would sigh fifty years later, Rita, less hard, in any case, than in Plovdiv; for Ruse, the third city of Bulgaria, received favorable treatment thanks to the personal friendship between Fiko Levi—ex-president of the Jewish community and member of the underground consistory—and the new deputy chief of police, Tsonkov, a man easily corrupted. Three hours of freedom a day, in comparison with only two in Plovdiv, an active black market making it possible to organize little parties, the authorization to form Jewish orchestras, to organize concerts for the community. One day, some young Bulgarian boys attacked your brother Tico; he was then wearing the star, while you were still too young. On the other side of the hill were your Jewish comrades. But you are leaning, Rita, on your brother's arm. You won't let him escape for fear of being abandoned. Even today in New York you tremble when remembering your fear, your shame at being a Jewish child.

On 28 August 1943, just back from a secret visit to Berlin, Boris III suddenly dies. The anti-Jewish legislation is struck down.

Now back in Sofia, the Vradjalis lived on Bratia Miladinovi Street. Between 1939 and 1945 three thousand Jews emigrated from Bulgaria to Palestine. Between 1948 and 1949, thirty-five thousand; you were among the latter. Sofia was a cradle of Zionism, with Marcou Baruch at the head of Bulgarian Zionism; he established a French journal in Philippopolis to encourage emigration.[4] Similarly, numerous colonization associations close to the Lovers of Zion—Hovevai Zion—had been formed in various cities. Tsio Meier could have read *El Amigo del Pueblo* or *La Boz de Israël*. He could have been present at the passionate speeches of an Albert Romano, president of the Zionist movement, as well as those of Bernhard Arditti, the cousin of Elias Canetti, who lashed out at the atavistic superiority of the Sephardim, their mad pride in djudyo, promoting instead a return to the sacred Hebrew language. He could have been active in one of the leftist Zionist parties: Poaley Sion, Hashomer Hatsair. On 3 May 1924, in fact, the synagogal committee had established a new tax in support of Keren Hayesod, the Palestine Fund, created in 1920 at the Zionist Congress in London. Each contributor had to meet his obligations under threat of being denied entry to the synagogue and the right to Jewish marriages and funerals.[5]

However, none of that truly concerned you, I believe, nor was Israel ever for you the country where Jews would henceforth never be ashamed, a refuge against persecution, a homeland, even if you would be frightened one more time. Nor did you have any awareness of belonging to some kind of elite. No, this branch chose to live in Israel without returning to the Law of Moses. You returned as strangers to that country fashioned by the Ashkenazim, after the Righteous among the Nations had decided to return the Land of Israel to the Jews.

> For the dear land our fathers trod,
> Must we ever in exile keen?
>
> . . . .
>
> When, Zion, shall I see thy ramparts rise,
> And the gleaming tops of thy towers?[6]

The trip in the freighter lasted five days. Tsio Meier, who didn't know Hebrew, could not lay claim to any qualified employment, and agreed to work in a stone quarry supplying material for road construction. Vicky, with her knowledge of numerous languages, was able to take in refugee children from all over who streamed to the Land of Israel. She earned a dollar a day! Scarcely arrived, you had to change your name in order to satisfy Ben Gurion's doctrine. At the Czernowitz Conference they had decided that Hebrew was to be the official language, *Am ehad, safa ahat*, Vradjali became Barzilay! Primo Tico's version is a bit different: tired of hearing his name mangled by the chief warrant officer at the constant roll-calls in the army, he finally complied when he heard "Barzilay" in order to have some peace. If Tsio Meier's immigration was not linked to the Zionist ideal, but was rather due to disillusionment with communism, how do you explain his keen interest in the national ideal of Israel once he got to the country and became a fervent pioneer? Had he been sole master of the fate of the family, there is no doubt that the Vradjalis, excuse me, the Barzilays, would have become farmers in a *moshav*. But this was of absolutely no interest to Vicky, who managed to find an apartment in a modest neighborhood of Tel Aviv, on Alharizi Street. Tsio Meier died just nine years after your resettlement, in 1958, when he was hospitalized after falling from the fourth floor of a building under construction.

Abba was very proud of his Israeli nephews. Had they realized an old dream that he had never dared to entertain? "If I forget thee, Jerusalem, may my right hand wither!" The photograph of Rita, a young soldier in the Tsahal, the Israeli armed forces, had a prominent place on his desk. Once she had completed her military service, Rita won a scholarship to the United States. On her return trips from Tel Aviv to New York, Vicky always stopped over in Paris to say hello to Abba. She never forgot to bring the delicious handmade marzipan from a Hungarian pastry shop in Tel Aviv. It is she who gave me on my tenth birthday the little diamond that I still like to wear. Rita, still unmarried, also came frequently to Paris. Ima and Abba cherished her, spoiled her. Rozika used to take her to the fashion houses. Did she appreciate it? She was used to more simplicity.

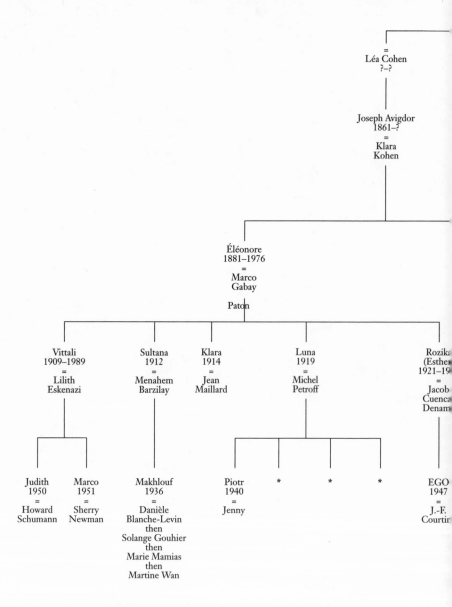

The Gabay *michpaha*

Only those persons mentioned in one way or another in the text are listed here by name.
Others are represented by an asterisk (*).

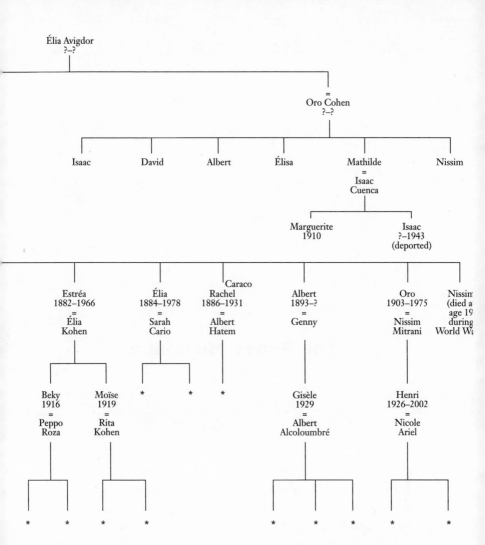

2

The Gabay Michpaha

In my grandparents' dark bedroom, above the conjugal bed, hung the portrait of Tsio Vittali in short pants, a hoop in his hand, his wavy hair falling onto his lace collar. Yet he was always bald when I knew him.

Al ijo bohor—Ya vino el ninyo! En bien sea venido!—the one whom Mamu on the advice of a Turkish sorcerer bathed in the Bosphorus in the light of a full moon in order to cure him of hemophilia, to Vittali, then, all privilege. He bore the Hebrew first name Haïm. His sisters had a right only to Turkish or Spanish names, except for Ima, who was clearly the most spoiled, hiding behind the odor of roses the biblical name Esther. A vestige of marranism? Probably because she was also born in the month of Adar. Vittali, did you used to recite the traditional morning prayer: *Benditcho seas Dyo ke no me fizites mujer?*

As the only son you also had a right to a room of your own, next to that of your parents, while the four daughters had to share the other bedroom, even sleeping two to a bed, paired by age. Luna and Rozika in one, Klara and Sultana in the other. You can imagine all the mad giggling!

Few memories of this uncle, except the Jewish holy days which were celebrated at his home from that day onward, since Mamu, now a widow, was too elderly to take on the very demanding ritual of Pesach, among others. A major cleaning of the house began two weeks in advance. The smallest crumb of bread had to be hunted down, to make sure that no particle of yeast was hidden in some crack—*o ke lo vide, o ke no lo vide / Siera amalgado kon el polvo della tyerra!*—eggs were boiled for whole days in flavored coffee grounds so that they would have a fine marbled color, *uevos jaminados*; the special service was taken out of the chest where it had been stored since the previous year; new shoes were bought, generally at A L'Aigle, rue d'Auteuil, since thanks to the Mundia office we had a discount there. From then on Vittali sat in the place of honor at the head of the table and read the Haggada, the history of the exodus of the Jews from Egypt.

Mamu monitored from the corner of her eye the preparations of her daughter-in-law, the *Chkenazia*: Hold on! What had Papu thought of that? He who claimed to be *sefarad tahor*. Didn't people use to say that the *Chkenazim* were not of the same race, that they were not *de mi pueblo*, that they were crude and dirty, the *Lejli*, the *Tudeskos*, weren't they mockingly called *Yidshy*, while we had preserved the "pure" Castilian of Cervantes? Weren't we superior to them? Poor Lilith must have been very poorly received by that army of quietly ironic sisters-in-law. It is true that she was *de buena familya*, everything *benadam*, she had studied in England, and became very devoted to her parents-in-law. Nor was there ever lacking the *haroset*, symbol of the earth that the Jews kneaded during their captivity in Egypt, nor the hard-boiled eggs, symbol of life, nor the *apyo* whose bitterness was to recall the misery of slavery, nor the sheep bone, commemorating the sacrifices from the time of the Temple of Jerusalem and the end of captivity. Marco, the youngest of the cousins, recited the *Ma nishtanah*, asking the questions: What does the unleavened bread signify? What do the bitter herbs signify? I don't remember whether we stood up at the end, as I have seen done at other sedarim, in order to dance and sing *Had gadya, had gadya . . .* a lamb. Perhaps because there were so few men in this family, and only men were supposed to dance and sing. This is why we didn't hear the celebrated "Kavritiko":

> *Un kavritiko ke me merko mi padre*
> *Por dos levanim, por dos levanim.*
> *I vino el gato i se komyo el kavritiko*
> *Ke me merko mi padre*
> *Por dos levanim, por dos levanim.*

> My father bought a little goat,
> For two cents, for two cents,
> The cat came and ate the goat
> That my father had bought
> For two cents, for two cents.[1]

But there was worse, Papu, than the mismarriage that you had to suffer with your daughter-in-law, Lilith the Ashkenazic. You managed to have tradition respected by first marrying Sultana, your eldest daughter, to one Menahem Barzilay, *de los muestros, de mi pueblo,* but the corporal, who received two citations, died fighting for France six years later, in June 1940 at Fresne-Mazancourt, leaving an orphan, Makhlouf, henceforth a ward of the state. You found him safe haven from the Gestapo—a small private school on rue Boileau, where he stayed as a boarder and where Ima and Abba out of gratitude enrolled me in the first grade. In your dark bedroom, on the dresser, the photo of Makhlouf, six years old, his head surrounded by curls. I don't remember playing with him, but he claims to have taught me the rudiments of reading. I remember his first wedding when from under the table I heard with delight the orchestra of his new brothers-in-law.

> *Sultana, reyna de ermozura,*
> *Sultanika, buen del padre,*

I tambien de la su madre.
A su padre le parese,
Oro fino i un diamante,
A su madre le parese,
Perlas karas i joyeles.

Sultana, queen of beauty,
Little Sultana is surely the daughter of her father
And just as much of her mother.
To her father she seems
Fine gold and diamonds.
To her mother she resembles
Costly pearls and jewels.

Luna, the third of your daughters, was the first to disappoint you, Papu, to undercut your upbringing. Luna, high cheekbones, so much gayer, more radiant than Ima in this photo that shows your last two daughters, seated on the arm of your leather armchair, fashionably dressed like twins. For you her birth was the occasion to test the proverb *Tres ijas i una madre, mala vida por su padre!* On the beach at La Baule that summer in 1939, Luna is frantically skipping rope, but Piotr sits firm—in her womb. Luna was married off quickly, so quickly, on 28 October 1939. No need to show the bed linen to prove her virginity in the eyes of the neighbors. *Tyene ijas, tyene ansyas.* What gave you the greater grief, Papu, Luna or the declaration of war?

How dark it was, the spring before the summer of 1942. On 27 April, Darquier de Pellepoix succeeded Xavier Vallat as the head of the Commissariat General for Jewish Affairs, establishing the National Club against Foreigners and the Association for the Defense of the Race. Bousquet was appointed Secretary-General of the Interior for the Police. On 29 May, despite the reluctance of the Vichy government and of Darlau, who feared that forcing the Jews to wear distinctive marks would arouse people's pity for them, the Germans imposed the wearing of the yellow star on the Jews of the occupied zone. Jews whose names began with A and B were to go and get the insignia at the police station in their neighborhood or district. Jews whose names began with the letters C to G had one day of grace: distribution would take place on Monday, 3 June. Three stars were exchanged for one point on their textile rationing card. The legal requirement to wear the star, over the heart, was decreed on 7 June.[2]

You had been of age for two months, Rozika. For you, as for Suzanne Kaych, the weather was fine that day, you loved the summer, you loved life, but unlike her you did not have to rebel nor to put together "with the cheap yellow and black stones of artificial jewelry an exact reproduction of the star that had been imposed" in order to mock the ordinance.[3] As a Turkish national, Rozika, you didn't have to bear the star of shame. Doesn't Bielinky note in his *Diary* for 3 June 1942: "The Turkish Jews, being from a neutral country, are not obliged to wear the insignia. A Jewish family showed up at the police station yesterday, the husband and wife didn't get badges, but they were given them for their two girls aged six and nine, both born in Paris and thus treated as French."[4] That time you were not made a pariah: after the disk, after the turban, after the hat, the star, too, is yellow. *Amariyo* is definitely your color. You did not wear the sign of infamy. You would not have had the humor of the marquis de Pombal who, once Joseph I of Portugal had declared that all Portuguese whose ancestors had the least bit of Jewish blood had to wear a yellow hat, appeared in court with three yellow hats under his arm, arguing that he didn't know a single prominent Portuguese who didn't have a drop of Jewish blood in his veins. The first hat was then intended for himself, the second for the Grand Inquisitor, and the third in the event that His Majesty himself wished to cover his head.[5]

You were relieved: you so badly wanted to belong to that French society, to be loved, to be one of them, rather than *de los muestros*. Didn't you study French at the Institut Notre Dame de Sion in Pangalti when the francophone and denominational schools opened again, before going on to the very middle-class Lycée Molière in the 14th arrondissement of Paris? Yet, Rozika, you thought that you were bearing the burden of your fathers on your frail shoulders; is that why your eyes were always so sad? Just as in Spain, five centuries ago, you could not speak the names of your parents or your grandparents without fear, or swear on the crucifix that you were not descended from Jews. Change your name? Change your religion? But on 10 June, the parishioners of Jewish origin of the Église Saint-Honoré-d'Eylau asked the curate to bless the badges that they nonetheless had to wear: "Our Lord Jesus Christ, if he were among us, would also have worn this insignia." Two children of Jewish origin, celebrating their first communion, accompanied by their families, wore the Magen David.[6] Hide the fact that one was Jewish? The sight of nuns always made you sentimental, you loved to say "Sister," and you could not pass in front of a church, a convent, or hear the sound of Catholic bells without trembling with emotion. My own tears, when on Christmas Eve you, exalted, sang to me, "Il est né, le divin enfant . . ." That evening I too would so much have wanted to be "one of them."

That 29 May 1942, you escaped your origins. But what happened, Rozika, that same day in your young girl's life, so that at your request or your father's (did he want to be certain of your virginity? to whom did he need to show that you didn't suffer from some family defect?) a prenuptial certificate was issued in your name?

Prenuptial Certificate
A. Akami
23 rue Nitot, XVIe
PASsy 16–00
PASsy 34–86
29 May 1942

I, the undersigned, professor of clinical medicine at the faculty of medicine, staff physician at the Broussais Hospital, Commander of the Legion of Honor, certify that I have examined Mademoiselle Rosie Gabay, twenty years of age [you had been twenty-one for two months!], residing in Paris at 4 rue Léon-Bonnat, XVIe, and have observed in her no symptom of any hereditary illness nor of any transmissible or contagious disease whatsoever.

I have issued this certificate at her request.

Paris, 29 May 1942

Your sisters seemed to regret on your behalf that you didn't play the assimilation card. You were, it seems, avidly courted; names were passed along to me: a famous physician, a famous surgeon, the one who operated on your nose. How had Abba been able to bear it? *Kyen tyene mujer ermoza, ke la tenga byen guardada!* But you must have been a bit jealous, you too, since one lonely evening you slipped into the conversation those fatal words: "You may have some little German brothers!"

On 19 and 20 July members of the French nationalist movement opened an exhibition on Jews and Masons in Nice. The hunt for the Jews of Paris began: Baltic Jews, Bulgarians, Dutch, Yugoslavians, Romanians, Luxemburgers, Belgians, residents of Danzig, Greeks—the raids succeeded one another at an infernal pace. On 22 July, after the roundup of Jews in the Vélodrome d'Hiver, Cardinal Suhard sent Marshal Pétain a letter of protest in the name of the annual assembly of cardinals and bishops. On 17 August, Chief Rabbi Kaplan asked Cardinal Gerlier, the Primate of Gaul, to intervene. On 19 August the cardinal sent a message to the Marshal. Between January and March 1943, the date of your "repatriation" to a neutral country, fifteen hundred more Jews would be arrested.

Klara, your second daughter, born on the last day of Hanukkah in 1914 or 1915, according to the calendar, apparently rebelled against your rules too, Papu. The struggle must have been long and pitiless; Ima kept a horrible memory of it. You turned your own daughter out of your home, you refused to feed the young couple in trouble—you violated the tradition of *meza franka*. Her sisters had to sneak left-overs from the family meal out through the courtyard window to her. By way of reprisal, Papu, you never offered Klara the drugstore of her dreams up on avenue Mozart. She ended up, however, marrying her Jean, a goy student who was a gifted painter, at the town hall of the 16th arrondissement on 30 August 1942, or fifteen days after the "Spring Wind" operation, the great roundup at the Vélodrome d'Hiver that involved twenty-eight thousand Jews. There were thirteen thousand arrests, and about one hundred suicides occurred. The day of her marriage, Sultana, her eldest sister, already in her dress for the wedding, called her:

"I can't be at the ceremony, the police are in the shop, they're arresting me."

After your marriage, Klara, you found Sultana at the Opéra police station, but they loaded her up to be taken to la Petite Roquette, then Drancy.

IV

DRANCY

If a man's not made of memory, he's made of
nothing. . . . You mustn't forget anything.
—Philip Roth, *Patrimony: A True History*

VI

I

The Return

Releases
Barzilay, Sultana, née Gabay, in 1912 in Constantinople, national-
ity Turkish, 167 boulevard du Montparnasse. Released from
Drancy on 2 March 1943.

Five other internees were freed that same day.
When were you interned at Drancy? At the end of 1940 or
1941, as you remember. Yet until 16 July 1942, with a few ex-
ceptions, the so-called delinquents, women were not subject to arrest.[1] I had to make an inquiry at the Archives of France in order to
fill the gaps in your faulty memory. But you doubtless had no desire
to remember that episode which, for many, sounded the death knell.

You had escaped the huge roundup at the Vélodrome d'Hiver ordered by Laval, following which the thirteen thousand detainees were transported to the camps of Pithiviers, Beaune-la-Rolande, and Drancy. Your respite was of short duration. You had been arrested on the orders of the German authorities on Sunday, 20 August 1942, the very day that Monsignor Théas, bishop of Montauban, had read from the pulpit a pastoral letter protesting the "violation of the most sacred rights of the person."[2] Earlier, on 23 August, Monsignor Saliège, bishop of Toulouse, had also reminded parishioners in his pastoral letter, despite a police prohibition: "Jews are men and women. . . . They are members of the human race, our brothers like so many others. A Christian may not forget this."[3] On 26 August, however, nearly four thousand persons were arrested.

You were freed a first time on 29 September 1942. In the police file of persons, your profession was listed as "blouse-maker" and your number in the central registry was 24-483. Your Jewish file number was 20-274. But in the police file of families, on the other hand, you had no profession, but were "war widow 39-40," and, under the heading "Disabilities," you had the care of a child: Makhlouf, born 19 March 1936, of French nationality.

In August and September 1942, there were no fewer than three shipments a week of one thousand internees, on Mondays, Wednesdays, and Fridays: the resident rolls department drew up lists of those who were to leave on the instructions of French inspectors, who received orders from the German police.[4]

You liked to smoke, and you had to pay thirty francs for each cigarette you puffed. You were lighthearted, carefree, and you probably didn't have time in the course of that month of internment to give any credence to the claimed destination of those voyages: German propaganda and nothing more! You would not have known of the death of Benjamin Crémieux during deportation on the pretext that "he was not of the master race." But you still had time to see the daily dead—by suicide or natural causes—done up in wrapping paper from which only the head showed, loaded onto a little handcart that two Jews, flanked by two inspectors, took from the camp to the Drancy police commissariat and then to the shack that served as a morgue.[5]

How and why were you freed? No doubt your Turkish nationality protected you, but since your husband, Corporal Barzilay, had been killed at Fresne-Mazancourt on 5 June 1940, you had also become a "head of family." What had this tsio been doing in that war, anyway? He had enlisted so that he would not be treated as a "filthy, malingering Jew," you claimed. Tsio Menahem thus joined the sixty thousand Jews who were in the French army. As during World War I, foreign Jews had enlisted in huge numbers, sixteen thousand of them succeeding in enlisting for the duration of the conflict, despite the obstacles thrown up by the administration. A number of them hoped thereby to obtain French nationality.[6] After spending six months in boot camp in Bacarès, Menahem telephoned you, Sultana:

"We are leaving for the Somme . . . no, I can't come and see you."

In May 1940 battle raged between the Somme and Alsace. Did he belong to the 22nd regiment, half of which was composed of foreign Jews, and which was given a national citation? Was he one of the thirty-six Jews of the 21st regiment who were decorated between 24 May and 14 June? At Mazancourt, in the space of an afternoon, sixty soldiers of the 22nd regiment were killed, fourteen of them Jews. Perhaps it was 5 June. You had no more news, Sultana. You looked for your husband for six months, and you put an advertisement in the local newspaper in the Somme region. The mayor responded that Menahem had been buried in a wheat field. Vittali, your elder brother, left with Klara to claim the body of his brother-in-law.

Now here you are interned at Drancy again, Sultana, on 21 November 1942! Probably you had begun again to frequent the bar at La Coupole after the curfew. Four months of renewed internment, that must have seemed long. November, December, January, February: your little boy had to wear the yellow star after his sixth birthday in March 1942. Your sisters, on the other hand, being either Turkish citizens or married to Frenchmen, were exempted.

In reprisal for an attack carried out against a brothel patronized by Wehrmacht officers in Marseilles on 24 January 1943, Hitler ordered fifty thousand residents of Marseilles to be sent to concentration camps and the buildings of the Old Port to be razed. There were twenty thousand arrests. The prisoners were transferred from Gurs to Drancy before leaving for the east. Laval proposed to strip the citizenship of all Jews naturalized since 10 August 1927. On 30 January came the creation of the militia: antisemitic persecution, the battle against the Freemasons, the hunt for communists, all this intensified. On 16 February, six hundred thousand young Frenchmen were affected by the law and the decree introducing compulsory labor service. March 1943 saw a slackening in the pace of the series of deportations. By 2 September 1943, once Convoy 59 had left for Auschwitz, there were only 646 internees left.[7]

You were no longer there. Since you were freed on 2 March 1943, Papu had only nine days to get you on board the last convoy leaving for Turkey, along with Rozika and Makhlouf, whom he had got entered on your passport. You were then part of the three thousand Jews who, thanks to the intervention of their embassies, could be repatriated to neutral countries or German allies (Italy, Hungary, Switzerland, Turkey).[8] Tsio Albert Avigdor, Mamu's brother, his wife Genny, and their daughter Gisèle looked after you on the way. Papu and Mamu, for their part, counted on joining you later. Your sisters, married now, remained behind, one in Normandy, the other in Paris, sending supplies to Vittali, who was hiding out in Villa Flora with his Corsican mistress. You claim that the train was armored and that you had taken along food for eight days.

Cousin Becky in Jerusalem remembers: "One day Uncle Merkado said that he had to leave for Paris because of the children, in order to give them a better education. . . . They came back because of the Great War, and we spent some very fine times together."

On 11 March 1943 the consulate general of Turkey issued you, Rozika, a passport in order to "return" to Turkey, not one of the warring parties. You and our family had arrived in France in 1931. You had had the wisdom to remain "Turkish subjects." You were very lucky: on 30 January 1941, in fact, a Turkish law was passed prohibiting the granting of resident or tourist visas to Jews who were being sought in their country of origin. In the early 1930s Turkey had put in place a policy for the selective admission of Jewish refugees. Thus, in 1933, on the occasion of the reform of the University of Istanbul, the government received forty German Jewish academics from among those who had lost their positions in Germany, but there was still no question of extending this measure to all those who were victims of Nazi persecution.[9] You, Rozika, were very lucky to have renewed your passport in time, very lucky not to have left Turkey with your family before 1931, for those who had not come back between 1924 and 1927 could not benefit from the "return" policy, witness your Salti cousins who had been resident in France, in Sète, for a long time and who thus became stateless.

Consulate General of Turkey
Passport
Valid for One Year

Issued by the Consulate General of Turkey to Turkish citizen Roza Gabay for travel to Turkey and all other countries.

Ismi (name): ROZA GABAY
Babasinin Adi (father's name): Merkado
Dogdugu yer (place of birth): Istanbul
Dogdugu sene (date of birth): 1337/1921
Pasaportu aldigi yerdeki ikametgahi (residence): Paris
Gidecegi yer (destination): Turkey
Seyahat sebebi (purpose of trip): *avdet* (return)

Paris, 11 March 1943
(currency export authorization: 5,000 francs, 16 March 1943)

You did not have time, Rozika, to see the great department stores, the luxury shops, the florists, complying with their unions for the removal of showy or expensive items from their windows. You hadn't got wind of the distribution of antisemitic tracts that the Popular French Youth movement organized in the 15th arrondissement of Paris on 2 April, nor of the brawls of 17 and 20 March in a café on the corner of rue Sedaine and rue Popincourt. You were not present in June for the closure of the bakeries for lack of bread. You didn't know about the shortage of meat in September and October, nor the experience of exchanging old rags or clothes for textile ration points. But you must have been a witness to the raids in Marseilles in January, those on children in the homes of the General Union of the Jews of

France (UGIF) in February, those of 11 and 20 February when sixteen hundred Jews of all ages were interned at Drancy.[10]

You must have arrived in your native city, Rozika, in the company of Sultana and Makhlouf, around the month of May. You remembered hardly anything of the Turkey of your childhood, and no doubt like Rita Frances you left a boyfriend back in France.

Prima Rita Frances also embarked for Turkey, two months before you. War broke out when Rita was on holiday. Her father, Victor, urged his family to remain in Beaulieu-Villefranche, then they withdrew to Nice for a year. This was the time of the phony war. They returned to Paris. The census came: Victor spontaneously went to the Montrouge police chief, Monsieur Dumarchais, to complete the formalities, but the latter, who had known him for a long time, refused. At Victor's insistence and in annoyance, he finally gave him the forms. Victor, protected by his embassy, filled them out conscientiously and submitted them. The police chief tore them up. "One of the righteous," today remarks Buby, Victor's son, then thirteen years old.

There was another: the man who three times in a row sent away Hélène Cuenca, Jacky's wife, who had also wanted to register, for he couldn't believe that with such a pretty face and not a trace of accent, Hélène, born in Warsaw, was a Jewess! Hélène's father, Chaïm Israel Kaufman, arrived when she was not expecting him. His daughter, after taking a long look at him—blond, blue eyes, straight nose, only a slight accent—went back to see her policeman.

"What is your nationality?" she asked him.

"French!"

"And mine?"

"French too."

She then asked him to enter on her father's ID card the notation "French." Chaïm became Charles, still Kaufman, a tailor. Some months later her mother, Dora Finkelstein Kaufman, arrived with her little sister of nine. After another trip to the police station, everyone ended up with French ID cards!

On 7 November 1940, the Frances were getting ready to leave their apartment in Montrouge to withdraw to Sète, where a related family, the Bensassons, were settled. The Germans, alerted to events—who had turned you in?—were on the landing. The father, Victor, explained their departure due to the material difficulties that he faced because of his wife's tuberculosis and his care of the two children. Djemille had, in fact, been obliged to spend two years in a sanatorium in Switzerland, while the children boarded at a school in Beauvais. The Germans insisted: did religion really have nothing to do with this hurried departure? Victor stood up to them: he was a free thinker and, moreover, in possession of an *Ausweis* in due form. Finally, exasperated, he reached in his pocket and removed a business card from Goebbels, the minister of propaganda, who had ordered the Louis Martin bindery, where Victor worked in Montrouge and which had been requisitioned for the war effort, to print a work entitled *The Collapse of the West*, a printing job that Victor had done his best to sabotage! The Germans had to back down.

In November 1942, Victor Frances, whose two applications for naturalization as well as his enlistment had been refused, on the pretext of the bad hip from which he suffered, took steps to return to his native country with his family. The expedition lasted a month and a half in a train filled with Germans. They had been able to leave with all their baggage, pieces of gold sewn into the hems and collars of coats or hidden in the heels of shoes by a clever shoemaker on Boulevard Richard-Lenoir. At the stopover in Milan, a cousin, a certain Michele Cuenca, who did not have the good fortune to please the pretty Rita, asked for her hand in marriage. Trieste: there she could perhaps have met Klara and Joseph Avigdor, Rozika's grandparents, if they were still there. Zagreb: Croatian partisans fired on the train; terrified, they lay on the floor. Sofia: Tsia Vicky and Tsio Meier, her cousins, as we have seen, took them in. Sofia was occupied by the Germans. Rita remembers a city with torn up streets, worse than in Istanbul, the rain, mud, cold—she's wearing a fur coat in the photograph from this stage of the trip—and especially the "pyramid cake" that she greedily ordered in a tea shop.

2

From the Partisans to the Camps of Upper Silesia: Robert

ohor Frances and his wife Sarina, née Cuenca—one of the
daughters of Nono Salomon—having left Turkey in their
turn, arrived in France in 1928 to join members of the family
who had already settled there. When World War II broke out, Robert, their grandson, his sister Vivette, and their mother, Allegra (all
three born in Brusa, the first capital of the Ottoman Empire), after
having discussed the matter together, decided not to seek repatriation to Turkey. When your adopted country is in danger, shouldn't
you come to its aid? Robert, preparing for his advanced examination
in philosophy, was soon active within the Franc-Tireurs et Partisans
(FTP), a resistance movement that had emerged from the French
Communist Party in August 1941. He was then living in the Auteuil
quarter of the city, in an apartment which, on loan from Henry Ray-

mond, had become a place where tracts and posters for the National Student Front were produced. Allegra, for her part, was not affiliated with a resistance movement, even though she lent her support to the student organizations and then to the FTP. After taking refuge in Montargis with Henry Raymond's parents, she visited her children who had remained in Paris once a month.

Early one morning in June 1943, three members of the Gestapo searched the apartment. Out of bravado, Robert played a few notes from the prelude to Wagner's *Tristan und Isolde* on the piano. The Germans, thinking that it was a call for help, tackled him. An identity card they found under the pile of sheets freshly stacked in the linen cupboard, which had since September 1940 carried the terrible compulsory red "J" stamp, incriminated them even more. Robert and his mother were imprisoned in the male and female facilities at Fresnes, under a double accusation: resisters and Jews. On 6 August, when they were waiting to be shot at any moment, Robert was transferred to rue des Saussaies. He would be tortured by the security forces of the German occupiers who extracted a false confession from him: "I was a member of the National Student Front. I distributed some tracts. I do not know who gave them to me. I don't know the name of the people."[1] The threat was always the same: you will be shot. He was taken back to Fresnes, but he would thenceforth be in solitary confinement, in a cell marked G (*Gefährlich*, "dangerous"). He would find consolation in a book of prayers, intended for prisoners, which provided him with "spiritual exercises." Robert, in the course of the interrogation, would cry out: "Jesus, my arms, my arms" to the great stupefaction of his torturers. "Jesus, you too are a Jew!"[2]

Robert didn't know that his mother was also being kept in solitary confinement at Fresnes. He was afraid that she had cursed him for having led her into this hell. In the absence of a mother figure, the protecting image of Mary offered recourse: he converted to Christianity. *En este mundo sufrymos por ser djizyos, en el otro sufriremos por no aver sido djizyos?*[3] Robert met his mother again in September 1943, a chance meeting in a corridor of the camp at Drancy. Since November 1942, the detainees could move about freely within the camp.

It was on 20 August 1941 that the future city of La Muette, that horseshoe-shaped block of low-rent apartments, still under construction, opened its gates as the transit camp that would see some eighty thousand Jews of all nationalities pass through before 17 August 1944. Detained there were foreign Jews who had naively gone to have their expired ID cards renewed, sick Jews who had been taken from hospitals, all those who had been condemned by a French court, however minor the infraction, those who had been apprehended in public, and, lastly, those who had been arrested for violent acts of resistance. All that these French detainees, foreigners, former resisters, or others had in common was the fact of being Jews. From August 1943 on, more and more French Jews, until then "privileged"—and now developing an extreme xenophobia with regard to foreign Jews, whom they blamed for their lot—were interned there.[4] Compared to Fresnes, Drancy seemed a haven to Robert.

Drancy, September 1943: truly a haven? Admittedly, from 1 April 1942 to the end of that year, 1,191 Jews were freed, and an additional 406 before 1 July 1943. Admittedly, there was a slackening in deportations after the terrible month of March, when five thousand Jews from the southern zone were deported to Drancy. April, May, and August 1943 had in fact been rather "light" months with no deportations, when concerts were even heard in the camp, when the children had a right to a circus performance, when an underground correspondence network was established. Admittedly, the deported were no longer searched or had their heads shaven; they were able to keep their baggage and were given a blanket, underclothes, and shoes furnished by the Union Générale des Israélites de France (UGIF)—so much material to be confiscated on their arrival in Auschwitz. Similarly, they were given a receipt for their money, which would be reimbursed, they were assured, in zlotys on their arrival. But during that dark year there were new arrivals in February, April, and July, the ill who had been hospitalized in the Rothschild facility; in March, the foreign employees of the UGIF; then in July, its administrators; and in September, institutionalized Jewish mental patients.[5]

Drancy, September 1943, a haven. Poor Robert! On 9 June, however, Aloïs Brunner, Röthke, and his deputy Ahnert arrived there. This would be the nineteenth camp directed by Brunner, the same person who had ravaged Salonika in February 1943, and to whom your cousin Isaac Cuenca had fallen victim.[6] On 2 July 1943 the Germans officially took over the operation of the camp, and in September German troops were deployed on the Mediterranean coast, hunting down Jews who had followed the withdrawal of the German Fourth Army: "A more favorable occasion to proceed to a complete purification has never presented itself before," wrote the director of the investigation and control division (SEC) for the southern zone[7] to the Commissariat General for Jewish Affairs.[8] Rumors of deportation were amplified, packages and even mail were suspended, with the exception of the internees' arrival letter and the one they had a right to send just before being deported, both intended to provide the Germans with the addresses of their families.

Just like the others, Robert, you were obliged to stop dead still when you met a German, fade like a shadow into the wall when he walked up the stairs. Did you know German? All the signs at the camp were in that language. Did you receive a slap from Brückler, Brunner's second-in-command, for having worn dark glasses?[9] Aloïs Brunner multiplied the categories of deportable persons, French Jews no longer being protected by their citizenship. Did you hear of that new destination, the island of Aurigny, Devil's Island, to which, two months before your arrival, seven hundred internees were sent in July 1943? On 3 July 1943, André Baur wrote to Albert Manual concerning the new regime at Drancy. The president of the central consistory and the chief rabbi officially alerted Laval and Pétain on 12 July. The French Communist Party distributed a tract entitled "The Truth about the Drancy Camp" and the hellish conditions there were described over the BBC broadcasting service.[10]

Perhaps, Robert, you hoped to escape, as did ten of the eleven deportees in a convoy that left on 9 February 1943, or like the eight others on the 13th of the same month. Did you know that nineteen escapees from the convoy of 20 November had begun to dig a tunnel at Drancy in the middle of September—you were already there— right under the office of the Jewish commandant, Robert-Félix Blum, who pretended to see nothing, hear nothing? Arriving from Compiègne to Drancy in May 1943, Robert-Félix Blum, a factory owner and former military officer, cooperated zealously with the Nazi authorities and was promoted to internal commandant of the camp. He would be dismissed from his functions on 11 November, the very day of the discovery of the tunnel on which seventy men, working in three eight-hour shifts a day, had been engaged, and he himself would be deported in the last boxcar on 17 August 1944.[11]

Drancy, September 1943, a haven . . . You could not have known of the last instructions given by Robert-Félix Blum in a "strictly confidential" internal memo, "In the event of transport to the east," sent to the staff supervising the deportation planned for 7 October, precisely the one of which you would be a part. "The truck requisitioned for the transport of foodstuffs to the station will also transport mattresses, buckets, stairwells, and metal stripping. It will return the morning of departure to bring the material back to the camp." Prisoners were organized by the stairwells they regularly used. Blum had meticulously foreseen everything: "For the departing stairwells, wake-up call and coffee are set for 4:30 A.M. tomorrow, 7 October 1943" (this was two and a half hours earlier than in the day's timetable set by him on 16 September 1943). Stairwells 1 and 2 will begin to come down at 5:15 A.M."[12] For this convoy, Brunner telexed Eichmann on 30 September, asking him for a green light for the departure of a convoy on 7 October (XLIX-49). On 1 October Eichmann replied favorably (XLIX-51), adding that a commando unit to escort the convoy would be coming from Stuttgart. The usual telex (XLIX-52) was signed by Röthke. It states that on 7 October at 10:30 A.M. a convoy of one thousand Jews left Paris-Bobigny with Meister der Schupo Schlamm as officer in charge of the escort party. Two members of the same family already at Drancy: how had your sister Vivette escaped the "family consolidation" that Brunner had planned? A thousand companions in misfortune—more precisely 564 men, 436 women, and 800 children under eighteen—left Drancy at the same time you and your mother did, in Convoy No. 60. Your *Abtransport* clearly indicates your rank in this iniquitous lineup:

266. FRANCES, Allegra: 15-12-91. *Seamstress*. 4632.
267. FRANCES, Robert: 4-12-19. *Student*. 4633.[13]

Also bearing your family name was an "Olga: 1-1-18" coming from Rhodes.

You doubtless had, Robert, no precise idea of what was waiting for you. The eastern European detainees had a name, *Pitchipoï*, for your destination, a mythical name no doubt invented by the internees to reassure the children who were leaving as well. *Pitchipoï*, that word whose origin no one knew, did not evoke any "precise image, resonating like an eternal curse, the site of the pogrom or the ghetto."[14]

On 13 October, Höss, the commandant at Auschwitz, telexed Röthke that on 10 October at 5:30 A.M. the convoy had arrived as ordered (XLIX-53). The voyage in filthy boxcars without straw, bread for three days thrown on the floor beside the latrine buckets, had lasted three days and three nights. On the loading dock at Auschwitz, you were assailed by the vision of "extra-terrestrials" dressed in gray and blue striped pajamas, wearing hats of the same material with polygonal crowns, suggesting "the entry into a world outside the ordinary where things one had never seen could happen."[15] On arrival, 340 men (with numbers 156940 to 157279) were selected and assigned to the construction of the Buna factory for synthetic rubber at the Monowitz work camp, which was administered from Auschwitz. You were one of them, Robert, and you never wished to erase your number.

Robert and his mother were separated, but they didn't yet know that it would be forever. Frances, Allegra: 15-12-91. *Seamstress*. 4632. Were you really a dressmaker? Allegra, daughter of Jacob Russo and Esther Soncino, was, however, the only one of the three girls in that family to study at the Alliance Israélite Universelle in Paris, from which she graduated with an advanced certificate. As a graduate, she owed the Alliance ten years of teaching. She taught in Bursa, where she became directress of the school. At the beginning of the century the majority of the thirty-five hundred Jews of the community were either cloth merchants or moneychangers and moneylenders possessing substantial capital, having occupied a huge sector of the bazaar since the end of the nineteenth century. Isaak Frances, Allegra's future husband, was a silk merchant. No doubt he benefited from the intervention of the Jewish community in 1899 when it lobbied the inspector for public debt in order to obtain the right to spin and weave silk at home, the monopoly for which had until then been in the hands of Greeks and Armenians.[16]

It was a Tuesday at two in the afternoon when Allegra—a bit tired from the voyage whose expenses, amounting to 7,600 Turkish pounds or 162 French francs, she had been recording since leaving Rhodes—arrived in Bursa, where she was to take charge of her class the next morning. She observed her little world in the school yard, wishing to make a good impression on her charges. How was she going to interest these children "who generally heard French spoken only at school"? Herself fresh from a Parisian boarding school without the advantage of any practice teaching, she feared that her French was too academic, too elaborate.[17] On 1 November 1911, Allegra wrote her first letter to the president of the AIU. She had just taken up her duties, was full of zeal, and hoped to affect favorably "the souls and minds of the children confided to her care."[18] On 19 April 1914, after three years of full-time teaching, she wrote that she deplored the poor aptitude of the girls for mathematics. Their day-dreaming and lack of energy compared to the boys are not the only reasons: "Since their parents still don't have the habit of making their daughters work in their offices or firms, . . . they find it useless for these future housewives to waste their time calculating the number of liters of wine or the weight of ingots."

Allegra departed in the column of future gas victims, Robert in the column heading to the Monowitz labor camp. Trying fifty years later to reconstruct the thoughts of those wan, terrified women who shuffled up the awful ramp at Birkenau, Robert imagined his mother's intention: "I will tell them that I was a teacher of French in the East. That experience, even here, might be of some use to me, who knows?"[19] Today Robert knows that Allegra was gassed the very day of her arrival.

Ay, madre mia kerida, from now on it is in the archaic language of your childhood—the tongue chosen by your ancestors when, fleeing Provence and the kingdom of Philip the Fair, they went into exile in Spain, while waiting to be forced to leave once again or to convert—that you will henceforth evoke Allegra, she who incarnated joy, whose lullabies still rise on your lips.

In captivity, you managed under cover to read Marx and Lefebvre. When you returned, you joined the Communist Party with little reluctance. This was a matter of duty for a former member of the FTP, since resistance and revolution went hand in hand during those years.

On 18 January 1945, this camp in Upper Silesia was evacuated, the prisoners moving, initially on foot, toward the camp at Gleiwitz. Once they reached Nikolai, it was a nine-day trip in open railroad cars that awaited the two hundred prisoners. They ate snow, they sat on their companions, they killed one another for a few crumbs of bread thrown to them by Czech workers. Kill to survive. *Die Toten heraus!* "Out with the dead!" the Nazis shout. Forty-three are counted out. The Russians are advancing: they are at Gleiwitz, at Breslau. Robert begins to hope for liberation, to think about the notes he had taken to prepare for his examination in philosophy. Provided that the student to whom he had entrusted them had not been arrested as well! The train advances from Prague to Dresden. The Oranienburg camp is full and cannot receive them. It would be at Flossenburg, then in Bavaria that the prisoners are put to work in March repairing the airfields bombed by the Americans as well as building a camp near Gannecker in Lower Bavaria. Abandoned by their jailer, Robert and a few of his companions in distress find refuge at a farm near Landshut. In 1990 Robert would try to relocate the compassionate farmer's wife. Landshut was already occupied by the Americans. The laughter of the GIs at the appearance of this skeletal old man of twenty-four still pierces Robert's heart today.

June 1945: a military plane to Le Bourget repatriates the 31 survivors of the 1,168 who left in Convoy No. 60. They go next to Lutetia Hall in Paris, which had been converted into a reception center. For Robert: the vain wait for Allegra, who was neither of the two women to escape, the reunion with his sister Vivette, the indefinite repression of an account of the atrocities he experienced, the refusal of any commemoration, the engagement in the present.

3

Bayonne and Its Jews:
Marie and Fortunée

Marie, Fortunée, and Rose, three of the seven children of Élise Cuenca and Moïse Salti, had also left Turkey for France in the 1930s. Rose studied at the college in Beauvais and made friends there, but left again for Turkey. Fortunée had already been engaged to Isaac Halfon in Turkey, and Marie met David Bally in Biarritz. Finally, they all decided to settle in Bayonne, the Ballys at 1 Boulevard Jean-Jaurès, the Halfons at 4 Rue Gambetta. Isaac and David, the two brothers-in-law, became partners in a hat shop. Marie and David had a daughter, Rachel, nicknamed Nelly, born on 11 October 1932. Little Maurice, the son of Isaac and Fortunée, was born in 1940.

Why did they chose the southwest of France? Drawn to the Bordeaux region by the presence of coreligionists, the Navarese Jews clandestinely settled in Bayonne after the confirmation of the edict of expulsion from Spain in 1498, first of all prudently making themselves known under the name of new Christians and having their infants baptized. Soon, however, Henri II granted them permission to settle everywhere in the jurisdiction of Bayonne, granting them letters patent through the intermediary of their fellow countryman André Govéa. On 11 November 1574, Henri III signed new letters patent. But the jealousy felt by the first arrivals with regard to newcomers, who very cleverly contributed to the city's prosperity, was such that after 1597 all Portuguese not able to prove ten years of residence in the city of Bordeaux were obliged to leave. Henri IV even issued an order in January 1602 banning them from the jurisdiction of Bayonne, even though it meant their penetrating further into the kingdom. In any case, these letters patent were never implemented, the parliament of Bordeaux very justly noting that it was absurd to expel useful citizens from a province where they had been sent, in order to permit them to return to a province from which they had been expelled.[1] It is thus that in consideration of their skill in trade, Jews again benefited from the favor of the government of Louis XIV, as seen in letters patent of 1656 and 1658, investing more and more often in cod-fishing ships and even acquiring whalers.[2] Biarritz, at the gates of Spain, had replaced Saint-Jean-de-Luz, where the majority of new Christians had gathered until the fateful date of 19 March 1619, when Catherine de Fernandès was burned alive by the population of that town. Soon, however, sorcery accusations against Jews spread to Biarritz. Flight again became necessary, and refuge was sought in Bayonne. Jews of the Sephardic rite claimed to have a more noble origin than their German coreligionists, and they traced their origins to the tribe of Judah. Thus the community of Saint-Esprit-lès-Bayonne, coming from Spain, used to called itself *Nefutsot Yehuda*, that is, *los dispersos de Juda*.

In 1760, in his will, David de Fonseca-Chacon had set as express condition that his heirs emigrate to France.[3] Yet this was not your motivation, Marie, Fortunée, Isaac, David, since you had to enter the hat business. But, like those first emigrants from the Iberian peninsula renewing ties with Judaism for the first time in the seventeenth century, you still recited on the morning of *Tish ah b'Ab* the elegy of Paloma in old Spanish, while the master, for his part, read in Hebrew:

> *Criador hasta cuando*
> *Tu Paloma quedera enlazada*
> *En la red del lazador*
> *Pobre i privada*
> *De sus hijos, solitaria se queda*
> *Esclamando: Señor!*

> Oh Creator, until when
> will your dove remain caught
> in the net of the fowler?
> She is poor, bereft
> of her young, she remains in solitude,
> crying: Oh Lord![4]

Bearing witness to the constancy of your faith, the gentle dove languishes in a foreign land under the yoke of the enemy who tries to seduce her and turn her away from the true God to the profit of vain idols, and she sighs:

> *Alivia sus penas*
> *I consuela los corazones lastimados*
> *Junta los empujados*
> *Dispersos por las naciones*
> *I aproxima la redemcion.*
> *Señor, Señor, Señor!*
> *Solitario se queda*
> *Esclamando: Señor!*

> Relieve her pains,
> Console the hearts of the afflicted.
> Gather these poor exiles
> Scattered among the nations,
> and send them soon the Redeemer.[5]

Marie and David, on 11 October 1932 you presented your little Rachel to the temple. After having announced the offering, the officiating rabbi closed the ceremony with these wishes for the mother and child: *Por su buena mejoria i salida, por la buena mejoria de la senyora su madre, i la merced ke Dyos la delivro de todo malo* (May she thrive and be welcome in the world; may her mother recover well and let us thank God for having spared her misfortune).

On 19 April 1943 the occupation authorities proceeded with large-scale raids on Jews in Nîmes, Avignon, Carpentras, and Aix-en-Provence. In May 1943 the Jews of Bayonne received an order to withdraw to Pau, the departmental administrative center. They were authorized to bring their goods, money, and belongings, but "Turkish, Romanian, and Hungarian subjects are exempted from the evacuation measures." Marie, Fortunée, were you still Turkish subjects? The director general of the UGIF wrote from Marseilles on 17 May 1943: "The operation for the withdrawal of our coreligionists from the Bayonne region began on Wednesday, 4 May 1943 with the transfer of the elderly from the Israelite Hospice of Bayonne to the departmental hospital in Pontacq. Forty-two indigent persons or welfare recipients were taken to Viados, Espes-Underein, and Charrite-de-Bas in the north of the Basses-Pyrénées. On 8 May the withdrawal operation concluded." On 21 May 1943, André Baur, vice-president of the UGIF,[6] wrote to R. Lambert, director general of the UGIF for the southern zone: "Evacuation of the Jewish population of Bayonne. We have received your information concerning the reception of our coreligionists who have withdrawn and we ask you to thank your delegate in Pau who seems to have acquitted himself of this task most satisfactorily. . . . Drancy. Numerous persons arrested in your zone are still arriving in Drancy." On 7 June 1943, André Baur, who had paid a visit a month earlier to the mayor of Bayonne, pleads in a letter for "benevolence toward all those affected by the evacuation measures . . . beyond the demarcation line, on the order of the occupation authorities." He asks the commissioner general for Jewish affairs to consent to a dispensation in the conditions under which the monthly payments were made.

Marie, Fortunée, what were the circumstances of your arrest? The night of 10–11 January 1944, "the French police and the German police proceeded in the departments of Gironde, Les Landes, and Basses-Pyrénées with the arrest of all Jews, including French Jews, without distinction of age, sex, or circumstances."[7] That 10 January 1944—the very day of the assassination of Victor and Hélène Basch by militiamen from Lyon under the direction of Touvier—Maurice Duchont, the police chief at the station on rue Esprit-des-Lois, received his instructions at the security police headquarters (KDS), at 12:30 P.M.[8] A note, written in German, informs him of the arrest planned for 8 P.M. of all Jews in the department, with the exception of the sick who could not be transported. Maurice Sabatier combined the functions of police chief for Gironde and chief for the region. The Landes and Basses-Pyrénées (now the Pyrénées-Orientales) are under his authority. Maurice Papon—who claims to have entered the Resistance on 1 January 1943—is under his direct orders in his capacity of secretary general for the Gironde prefecture and is thus the number three person in the organizational hierarchy.[9] Chief Sabatier will attempt to postpone the operation by personally going to Bouscat but, at 9:30 P.M., they are obliged to carry out orders, no countermanding order having come from the French government.

This raid, the most substantial as concerns the whole of the Gironde department and for which the KDS had demanded the participation of the French police, was but one in a series, the last of which occurred on 20–21 December 1943, when eight hundred Jews, of whom seventy-nine were French citizens, were arrested by the German police, without the knowledge of the French police authorities, and were deported on 30 December. It was perhaps that night that you were arrested, Marie, Fortunée, Rachel, Isaac, David. As the police raid did not report the number of failed arrests, only 22 out of 473, among which two elderly men of seventy-six and seventy-eight years of age, all the Jews of the Gironde were collected in the synagogue, thus profaned and transformed into a detention site, at 213 rue Sainte-Catherine in Bordeaux. Some claimed that the chief rabbi, Joseph Cohen, had fled and taken refuge at the archbishopric of Bordeaux, a version of events denied by his children. You were then evacuated on 12 January to Drancy, piled in cattle cars, with a latrine bucket as your only baggage. "When they left, there were 317 elderly

Jews from the Gironde alone. For some unknown reason, a few old men were not arrested."[10]

You were then not part of those Jews deemed "interesting, holders of the Croix de Guerre, disabled veterans, wives of prisoners," like a certain "Mme Bibal" whom Papon, assigned to Bordeaux since June 1942, had demanded be freed or at least left in Merignac.[11]

Marie and Fortunée, the Memorial of the deportation of the Jews of France[12] has preserved the date and number of your convoy for Auschwitz:

Convoy No. 66, of 20/1/44
HALFON, ISAAC, 20-1-06, ISTANBUL
HALFON, FORTUNÉE, 02-01-12, BURSA

Your little Maurice, aged four, is not with you. He had measles and the Germans feared contagion. He was left in the care of neighbors. The activity report from the Investigation and Control Division in Bordeaux, dated 1 February, however, states: "Contrary to rumors, children were not separated from their parents."[13] Maurice survived and was taken in four years later by his Aunt Flora, the last survivor of the children of Sarina and Bohor.

BALLY, DAVID, 5-05-05 (=1905), ISTANBUL
BALLY, MARIE, 25-12-11 (= 1911), BURSA
BALLY, RACHEL, 11-10-32 (= 1932), BIARRITZ

It was the internee Georges Schmidt, number 1910, who succeeded Robert Blum, on 22 November 1943, as internal administrator of the Drancy camp, and he must have drawn up the list for this convoy, assisted by Emmanuel Langberg. He banned the "recreational evenings" at the camp as well as music in the rooms, but it is reported that children were sacred in his eyes. Yet little Rachel also left with Convoy 66, along with 220 other little companions, after having passed through the concentration center in Bordeaux.

You would have been in transit eight days to get to Drancy. For Suzanne Birnbaum, arrested 6 January 1944, in Paris, arriving the next day at Drancy, and deported in the same convoy as you:

Drancy, of which we had such a fear at a distance, was a joke of a camp once you were there. After three days, you found out how to work the system, communicate with the outside, and receive packages of all kinds. . . . If you accepted certain conditions, you could even delay your deportation for two weeks or a month . . . in order to leave with friends whose acquaintance you had had the time to make.[14]

Leaving in Convoy No. 66, for which the usual telex is missing, were 632 men, 515 women, and 221 children under 18.[15]

The records of body searches made at Drancy indicate the sum that you were carrying with you, Isaac:

> Halfon Isaak: 1) 5245 francs, 2) 2 U.S. dollars (Book 56/ 114/ 11304, 13/1/44)

You, David, on the other hand had nothing to declare.

The original *Abtransport* documents for your convoy, destination Auschwitz, list:

> 58. BALLY, David: 5-5-05, Merchant. 11301.
> 59. BALLY, Marie: 25-12-11. Shopkeeper. 11302.
> 60. BALLY, Rachel: 11-10-32. None. 11303
> ....
> 444. HALFON, Fortunée: 2-1-12. *None.* 11305
> 445. HALFON, Isaak: 21-01-06, *Merchant.* 11305.

Marie and Fortunée, perhaps you were taken, like Suzanne Birnbaum, to Lager B, the camp for workers, and then to Block 27, the worst of all, the dirtiest, where the most feared *stubawas* held sway, where enormous rats ate the bread from under your head at night. Another woman named Marie, a bunkmate of Suzanne Birnbaum, was assigned to the sewing shop: but it was not you, my little Marie, for this woman had the good luck to return alive in the company of Suzanne. Perhaps you worked with swamp commando group 22 or stone commando group 105. Did you have the time to beg like little Suzy, "Oh my God! see that I don't die. So young, just because I am Jewish. My God! those who are killing us without trial, without remorse, will they have a right to live? Why, my God, why?" Did you have the time to regret "not having been gassed on arrival at the camp"?[16] In 1945, there were forty-seven survivors, among them fifteen women. Fortunée was not of this bunch, nor was little Rachel. David, for his part, survived. He was repatriated on 22 June 1945. For him, life continued.

Abba, you for whom memory was sacred, you never spoke to me of your cousins Marie and Fortunée. You were so close to them, you must have had lots of laughs with them. Their sister Flora was very close to your own sister Régine, "the cream of the family," as she called her, and each liked to spend the night at the home of the other. Even when Flora left in 1920 to study in America, you continued to visit the youngest sister. I have a photo of you playing cards with Rose and her husband David Ajuelo. Well, so you used to play cards, Abba?

V

In French
Territorial Waters

Tu madre, kuando te pario,
I te kito al mundo,
Korason eya no te dio
Para amar segundo.

When your mother gave birth to you,
And brought you into the world,
She didn't give you a heart
To love another.
　　　　　—"Adio kerida," Judeo-Spanish song

I

A Wedding Night at the Péra Palas

Cousin Beky writes from Jerusalem: "Your mother, Rozika, the last-born, was very pretty. . . . She worked as a model. . . . Uncle Merkado found her a husband. We spent some very nice days together and once the war was over everyone left again."

You looked like a model, Ima! *Kyen mal mos kera!* Papu joined you in Turkey in September 1943. He had to find a husband for you quickly, a Jewish husband, the husband of his dreams: *El ke tyene ija de kazar i no la kaza, se kaza sola!*

These two, Abba and Ima, were married on 19 November 1945, in Istanbul, at the Beyoglü town hall. You had to be given a dowry: the last-born of four daughters, you alone benefited from this privilege. Papu sold the building that you had kept in Çiçli. The religious marriage, for its part, had taken place the day before, at Temple Zulfaris. Your *ketuba* is made out in Hebrew and in Turkish: "In the city of Istanbul, situated on the shores of a great sea, Sunday, 13 Kislev in the year 5706, according to custom," you, Yaakov Kohenka, son of the late Selomo, asked your young fiancée Rozi (Roza) Gabay, daughter of Merkado, Menahem, according to Jewish tradition and religion, to "Be my wife . . ."

By the same rights, according to Jewish tradition, you engaged yourself to work with faith and respect, to honor and nourish her, et cetera, "in the eyes of the whole world."

Your fiancée brought you as a dowry ten thousand Turkish pounds in cash, to which were added five thousand Turkish pounds worth of belongings: clothing, jewelry, bedclothes. You, Abba, added "of your own free will" five thousand pounds in cash, which brought the sum to twenty thousand Turkish pounds, that were yours by right. You also affirmed that everything that belonged to you "in the present and in the future in this world, belongings and property, all my possessions, including the shirt on my back" would go to your heirs. Lastly, you promised not to take another wife "for the duration of [your] marriage," and not to seek a religious divorce without the authorization of the community. Rozika, was your head plunged seven times in the water at the *mikve*? In commemoration of the destruction of the temple of Jerusalem, Yaakov, the new husband, broke a glass on the ground. *Mazal tov!* A shower of rice fell on you when you left the synagogue. *Eyos tengan bien i mozotros tambien!*

In the Galatasaray quarter was the Péra Palas Hotel, cosmopolitan, deserted. Paneling and woodwork from 1900. The odor of the Orient Express still floating in the air, a bit stale. The shadow of Agatha Christie hovers over room 411. In which room did you consummate your marriage? The laughing whispers of her sisters; Rozika was not a virgin. But you, Abba, in accord with Jewish religion, paid the young wife the sum of two hundred pieces of silver "which came to her by right for the price of her virginity." To pull the wool over her husband's eyes Sultana counseled her young sister to hide under the covers a little tobacco box whose lid when closed would be enough to imitate the sound of a defloration. *Banamelololo?* Abba at least had the raging of his blood cooled.

In Istanbul, that 1 May 1994, women were still wearing the *chador*. I had thought I would come back filled with memories, impressions. In fact, I had left filled with memories, with impressions that were not my own. I had only fleetingly found them again, a chance encounter in the street, in a pastry shop. Those that I brought back, twitterings of the Turkish language as spoken by women, sounds, smells of the Egyptian bazaar, calls to prayer from a loudspeaker, put a stamp on an Istanbul that had already been told, superposed themselves on it. Soon I would no longer be able to distinguish them. I had crossed on foot the bridge that links Europe to Asia. As early as Herder, the Jews were "that strange people come from Asia."

From one continent to another, I contemplated, fascinated, the Bosphorus at my feet, looking out from the terraces of Topkapi. That little suburban railway, was it the magic route of the Orient Express? Were the bridge of Galata and its little fish restaurants all burned? Where were the golden cupolas of the mosques of my dreams? Was it possible that I was confusing Jerusalem and Istanbul so that those two so different cities became one in my mind, so great was my unsuccessful desire to reach them. Would I know the same disappointment in Jerusalem?

Curiously, Abba is absent from the marriage photos. Rozika, in a wedding dress, poses alone, serious, without smiling, so ravishing, surrounded by her long train, by baskets of flowers, her wedding bouquet in her left hand, a glove on her right hand, her palm open, following the photographer's advice. Then with Papu, wearing a hat with a high crown and a fitted coat. He seems very moved, standing by the side of *la ija de las vejes*.

There was no honeymoon, and you left, Rozika, to live with your sister-in-law, Rébecca, in Ankara. Seated on the low wall of a terrace, in a negligee, your hair up, long earrings, you are smiling under an arbor, and you wrote "A souvenir from your niece, Rosa, the Ankariot." Your whole trousseau fits right in there: suits, lightweight coats, furs. Did you put it on show before the eyes of the neighborhood, as was the custom the Saturday before your marriage ? The same arbor. It is November; no jasmine or wisteria. Abba, a dark suit, soft hat, white pocket handkerchief and shirt, strikes a pose like Bogart. It seems, Rozika, that you were working at putting talc on his temples so that they would have that silver sheen that you liked so much. Abba was already thirty-seven, thirteen years older than you. Why had he waited so long for you?

Rozika, had they asked you your opinion—*mi padre me kazava i yo no lo savia*—or did the same misadventure happen to you as to Prima Rita Frances? The Menda family, who kept the Germans and Americans supplied with goats' wool socks—they used them to make explosives—and whom Bohor Frances had graciously looked after, offered to employ his son Victor as a clerk when he came back to Turkey during the war. A partner of the Mendas then asked for the hand of Rita in marriage, but she initially refused. But Victor blackmailed his daughter: "If you don't accept this suitor, I risk losing my job and your mother and little brother will suffer because of it." Rita held out, negotiating for a compromise, and finally gave in seven months later. It was an unhappy marriage: *A tu ijo ambezalo a ennadar i a tu ija a endetchar!* "Teach your son to swim and your daughter to suffer!" Was yours happier, Rozika? You were twenty-four years old, you were the last of the daughters, it was time. Abba, they said, courted you passionately: telegrams, bouquets of flowers arrived on the hour. Makhlouf was sent to serve as your chaperone against the attacks of Jacob. "He was always there at the wrong moment!" Abba used to joke. Jacob wore such soft silk shirts; he was so refined, westernized, you hoped. In short, you too capitulated.

Your dowry was the object of endless quarrels; witness your letters as a young wife scarcely back in France complaining about her mother-in-law, who drew more profit from it than you. *La nuera traye achugar de oro i de marfil, la suegra tyene syempre ke dizir!*

You had already had enough of my Nona, sweet Rebecca, *la suegra*.

> *Las suegras de agora*
> *Son gusanos de pare;*
> *Los malmeten a los ijos*
> *I los hazen pelear.*

Mothers-in-law today
are like worms in a wall;

>they maltreat their children
>and cause quarrels among them.[1]

She thought that she had been sacrificed; she had to suppress her young woman's desires in order to satisfy a demanding mother-in-law. Abba wanted to leave the conjugal home. Ima ordered him to tell his mother. But wasn't I already on my way? Abba, for his part, was divided between his filial love and his love for one who was and would all her life be no more than a "kid" in his eyes, just like the child that was to be born. Is this the reason why until I was thirteen I had to share the same room as Ima, the children's room in fact, both at home as well as on holiday? Often I would slip into my mother's bed, and we would fight, just like kids, kicking each other under the sheets. Then, Abba, you would open the door, like a good father, indulgent and complaining at the same time: "Hand play, churls' play." It always ended badly in fact, since Ima was stronger than I.

You clearly had not gone out of your way, Abba, to bury your bachelor life, as the letters from your unmarried friends testify. Ankara no longer holds any charm for them, they miss your laughter, their businesses are going badly. They reproach you, as soon as you were married, of behaving like a stranger with them; they envy your new situation and are looking forward to the celebration that will mark the birth of your heir. Is it all the same letter or more than one, written on the back of an unlikely ledger sheet. Ima was apparently practicing writing—unless she was rejecting—her new name:

Madame Rosie Quencat (what is this unknown spelling?)
Madame Rosie Quencat
Madame Rosie Quencat.

2

In the House of Jacob

A papa i a mama este ninyo es de su papa
a la caye le yevara, todo el bueno le comprara.

Of his father and his mother, this child takes
   after his father
They'll take him into the street and buy him
   all he wants!
                    —Children's song from Morocco

In the deserted east, the beautiful Esther was dying of boredom,
while Rozika was missing her parents and her sisters, all having
returned to France. She sends her sister Klara a large anthology,
L'Ame française à travers la littérature (The French soul as expressed

in literature) by R. Bady and J. Chevalier, with the following dedication: "To our dear little Klara, an affectionate souvenir from two exiles lost in 'sweet Anatolia,' Rosie and Jacques." You have already taken the French forms of your first names. Didn't one of the unwritten clauses of the *ketuba* stipulate a return to the land of your adolescence, to France?

Jacob and Esther conceived their child "in French territorial waters" off Marseilles harbor, Jacob liked to specify. I used to have fun counting back on my fingers, September 1946.

Marseilles, the great Sephardic city that had seen so many refugees pass through; Marseilles, from which Peppo embarked for America in July 1941; Marseilles, where Jacky Cuenca lived under a false identity; Marseilles, where Raoul, another of your cousins of whom you never spoke, Abba, was arrested in January 1943, when he ought to have left for Argentina with his family in 1942, had it not been for the violent opposition of Tsio Meier. Born in Salonika, a Spanish subject, like the rest of his family, Raoul Saporta was tortured at the sorting center in Compiègne, as both Jew and a Freemason. He had in fact established the Masonic lodge in Marseilles, just as his grandfather had done in Salonika. A member of a resistance network, he was also a card-carrying member of the Spanish Republican Party, which made his case even more serious. In Auschwitz, in Matthausen, his knowledge as an engineer led to him being assigned to a factory manufacturing shells. He took advantage of circumstances by engaging in acts of sabotage. The Nazis broke his legs, wrapped him in electrified barbed wire. An American bombing saved him just in time. Raoul was liberated on 5 May 1945. You could have visited him, Abba!

The engagement of Raoul and Nelly Cuenca, in March, 1933, had been a lavish event. The entire dispersed family had gathered at the Hotel Bohy, rue La Fayette. The wedding was celebrated in June 1934, at the town hall of the 9th arrondissement, at the synagogue, and at the Spanish consulate. However, Nelly did not, once the moment came, want to profit by the Spanish decree that would have permitted her to be "repatriated" to Spain along with her children, so sure was she that she would find her husband again after the war. Since Raoul was not one of the racial deportees, but a political deportee, she needed a pass in order to go and look for him at the Lutetia in Paris. A famous professor of medicine who was consulted took a thousand francs from her and advised, "You have seen him still alive. That's already quite a lot." But Nelly insisted that he live. When at the end of several months he could stay seated at the family table, he still had that reflex, which his frightened daughter still remembers, of putting his hands over his plate lest someone steal his food. Knowing a number of languages, Raoul served as interpreter between the Americans, German prisoners, and the various allied army corps that were in charge of the repatriation of deportees. An ardent and militant Zionist, Nelly assisted with the clandestine departure of a number of boats from Marseilles to Israel. After the war, she became the regional representative of the Women's International Zionist Organization (WIZO) in Marseilles.

Luna, the eve before Rozika gave birth, had told her about her dream: *la kriatura . . . dos grandes ojos pretos komo azeytunes de Volo.*[1] Ima and Abba had agreed on the name "Francis" when Dr. Ravina announced, "There is the long hair of a girl." At the birth of his fourth daughter, Papu, they say, fainted.

> *Una ija, una meraviya*
> *Dos, kon savor,*
> *Tres malo es,*
> *Kuatro ijas i la madre*
> *Mala vejes para el padre.*

> One daughter, it's marvelous,
> Two, it's delicious,
> Three, it's rather bad,
> Four daughters and their mother,
> A bad old age for the father.

At the birth of your only daughter, Rozika, you burst into tears. Yet Tsia Rika Cuenca, apparently overjoyed, sent the news around the world: *Al kiridu Jacob li nasiyo una ijika alma*—"the soul of a little girl has entered the house of Jacob." I was born in the month of May, *mes de Mayo.* For this Francis manqué, no *brit mila.* Nor did they sing *Hadas, hadas, hadas buenas ke te vengan* on the seventh evening after my birth, but people nonetheless drank great amounts of raki—the Nahmias brand, of course!—and they ate *abudaraho.* This birth was even the occasion for Mamu to write her one and only poem:

> The first of May
> Friends gather
> To celebrate together
> The first of May.
> Summer, with its presence,
> Comes to grant our wishes.
> On the grass of the meadow we run
> Making wishes,
> The roses are in bloom
> And happy days are here.
> In the middle of the woods
> Birdsong deep in the trees
> Let us add to his language
> The concert of our voices.

In the absence of the hoped-for Francis, a play that was all the rage then in 1947, starring Danielle Darrieux, was behind the name that they finally chose for me, although I would have preferred that it be because of Nerval. But for a middle name I got that of Rita— one more Rita!—masking, as a vestige of marranism or the fear of a new flood, the Hebrew name Sarah, that of my great-grandmother Nahmias.

Sarah, the beautiful wife of Abraham, whom he passed off as his sister when he came to the lands of Abimelekh, while she was really the daughter of his elder brother Haran and thus his niece. At my birth, the family circle wished my parents: *Anyos de vida ke le kontes!* Did not the biblical Sarah live to be 127? But her life was shortened by thirty-eight years because of her disputes with Abraham over their servant Hagar and her son Ishmael. A prophetess—did she not convert the women just as Abraham did the men?—Sarah could not conceive until God changed her name from Sarai to Sarah, and that of Abram to Abraham. The first of the matriarchs, she named her son Isaac, "he who will laugh," in memory of her reaction to the announcement of this miracle by Elohim: wasn't she ninety years old at the time? Just like the biblical Sarah, the only woman with the privilege of changing her name, Sara Cuenca was born a second time with a new name, a new personality.

Abba wanted to forget Cuenca in order to Gallicize the maiden name of his own mother, Nahmias. "Clever!" would comment the rabbi who was so unwilling to recite kaddish over Jacob's grave and who would always refuse to associate the two names at the synagogue for the *meldado*. Marranos? But they had only changed their name to "protect" me from a new murderous madness. *Zakhor!*—an enigmatic word, certainly. Perhaps, after all, Abba had asked me to remember, to preserve, only in order to repair the oblivion, the effacement of origins in the transcription of the family name. Ima and Abba also wanted to obtain French nationality. Conceived "in French territorial waters" off Marseilles harbor, but of parents who were Turkish subjects, I had thus not benefited from a right to citizenship by virtue of birth in France. The procedure was long and complex, as the documents I found attest:

Ministry of Social Affairs, 4 June 1957
I regret to inform you that it is not possible at the present time to make a decision in your favor. In fact, given the contents of your file, my staff have considered it indispensable that we solicit additional information about you that has not yet reached us.

Armand Fouard

Abba had underlined "additional information" and had written in the margin "from whom?" rather than "what kind?"

On 21 January 1955 the justice of the peace of the 16th arrondissement granted me French nationality. Your own followed in July 1957. You had to produce a character reference, testimony to loyalty, as well as make a deposition concerning assimilation. With the beautiful name of their village in Castile, Cuenca—terribly Turkicized as Kohenka—now abandoned with their choice to become naturalized

French citizens, Abba and Ima voted for the first time, drunk with joy and pride, in 1958. On 4 March 1959, you are, however, still citizens of the Republic of Turkey, as your certificate of nationality confirms; but what good is that, since the certificate states that it "may not be employed for travel in lieu of a passport"? It cost you, Abba, 1,410 francs. Regularly extended up to 4 March 1963.

"I remember" Villa Flore, and Mme Pujold, the concierge of the building next door who lived in a lodge a half-flight down covered in tiles from top to bottom and who made such pretty flower costumes out of crepe paper for the school festival on rue Boileau. I remember Mlle Meunier, who had always been the nurse, with the pockmarked skin. Dr. Blechman—the Drancy pediatrician?—who had me take the "roast chicken" position in his dark office on avenue de Messine, and who so often came up to me with huge needles to carry out countless paracenteses. Rozika took refuge in the washroom to escape my howls, Abba and Nona having knelt down beside me to hold me on the goatskin. I remember the scalding sea salt baths that I was subjected to as a cure for my overweight condition, Mamu warming my little behind with a lit candle so I would stop wetting myself. I remember "thepurefoodlady" (ladamedelalimenpur) with the sweet smile from whom Ima, not really underweight, bought the wheat germ that she sprinkled on her salads as a supplement. I remember the watchmaker Geoffrion on avenue Mozart, who made the medal that I sucked until it was worn, and my first wristwatch, with the yellow lizard-skin strap. The dry cleaners Camillaluéné (Camille Halu Aîné), the Villefayot butcher's shop from which, rascal that I was, I ordered so many false deliveries, the tripe shop on rue La Fontaine and the horrible smell of veal, liver, and brains that Abba so loved to have fried. I remember that after the war, my parents, recent immigrants, had engaged the former cook of a minister. I remember the balcony of Villa Flore where, fascinated, I spied on the "crazy woman" who was hanging out her laundry, a scarf tied in a point over her hair, a row of clothespins strung out along her nose. The salamander, the boat-shaped bed, the little wooden shelves, and the Red and Gold books, books from the Trilby series, too, that had been given to me when I was recovering from a long bout of pneumonia, one winter day when I had fallen into the pool at the Jardin d'Acclimatation. I remember the room of Nona Rébecca, who never went out without a veil and gloves, that inveterate poker player who used to gather Berthe, Grete, and Rachel in her room for endless parlor games interrupted only by eating *borekas, filas, kurabiyes,* and other pastries with poppy seeds. When I was very little I would slip into the room and spend hours at Nona's feet while she sang me Judeo-Spanish lullabies and would regularly give me a raw carrot marinated in vinegar and cumin, a *loukoum.* Rozika did not like her mother-in-law, la suegra, complaining that her husband preferred his mother to her, that he spoiled her too much compared to his wife, and she would threaten:

> *Mi suegra*
> *La negra*
> *Kon mi se dakileya*
> *Yo no puedo mas vivir kon eya*
> *Eya es muy fuerte,*
> *Mas ke la muerte,*
> *Un dia me vere sin eya.*

> My mother-in-law,
> The shrew
> Loves to tease me,
> I can no longer live with her,
> She is very strong,
> Stronger than death,
> One day I'll be rid of her.[2]

Nona had to leave for the hotel on boulevard Richard-Lenoir. Sundays, I would go up steps four at a time and throw myself into an armchair. We would smother each other in kisses, the week had been so long away from each other, and Nona would start again to stuff me with pistachios, big, lightly salted *molossol* pickles, tomato balls. Nona came back one night to Villa Flore, dead. We didn't have a telephone line of our own then, and our calls had to come through the concierge, Mme Quintanel. She had called us, and Ima, in her usual thoughtless fashion, said to me as she hung up, "Nona is dead."

I was seven. I didn't know what death was, but I had a light case of jaundice. On the funeral announcement you could read:

You are invited to attend the funeral of
Mme Salomon Cuenca, widow,
Born Rébecca Nahmias
deceased in Paris, 26 Shevat 5715
which will take place on Tuesday 2 February 1954
at the Pantin-Parisien Cemetery
We will gather at 10:45 A.M. directly at the
grave situated in the 114th division.
Metro station Porte de la Villette, then bus 152.

On behalf of:

M. and Mme Meier Vradjali and their children,
Dr. and Mme Jo Pappo,
M. and Mme Jacob Cuenca and their daughter,
M. and Mme Paul Jaulus and their daughter,
   her children, grandchildren, and great-granddaughter;
Mme Haïm Pappo, widow, her children, grandchildren, sisters,
   nephews, nieces, great-nephews, and great-nieces;
The Cuenca, Pappo, Nahmias, Policar, Frances, Yahni, Narr,
   Hayon, Yeroham, Bensasson, Behar, Salti, and Ajuelo families.
And from the entire family.
5, Villa Flore, Paris, XVIᵉ.

"We were a huge family, but today we're scattered all over . . ."
Nona, born in Salonika in 1883, had joined her son Jacob in France in 1946. From 23 September on, she held the card of an "ordinary resident," the validity of which had been extended to 23 September 1955. How about that, you could have ID photos taken in profile! After Nona's burial, which I did not have the right to attend, the house was suddenly full of cousins and aunts. There was even "godfather," the one who had given me a cute plush penguin when all the other little girls only had teddy bears. I called him "Nico." My penguin had a little pointed red felt hat topped with a button, a white stomach that I opened up several times to discover that he was

stuffed with horsehair, just like I used to unscrew the necks of my dolls in order to examine the working of the eyes better. In order to respect *los syete*, the seven days of mourning, Abba installed himself on a mattress on the floor. But whose clothes had the rabbi been able to tear as a sign of mourning? I don't remember whether my aunts Reginika and Vicky traveled to the funeral. Then the first month of mourning was over, *kortamos el mez*: thereafter Abba would punctually go each year to the Don Abravanel synagogue on rue de La Roquette, *por el meldado de maman*.

Still at Villa Flore: father's arrival, exhausted, late in the evening.
"Abba!"
"Ija del baba!"
"Do you want to box?"
And so they would box, for laughs.

English shoes with ankle straps, white or yellow Dédé socks, white topstitched gloves with that terrible pressure on my pulse, I went up avenue Mozart with Ima. "Would you like to have a little brother?" Why that violent denial, that flush that spread over my cheeks, that heart that was suddenly beating wildly, why that feigned indifference when Ima admired a baby in the garden, caressed the hair of the flock of the children of the dressmaker who was regularly pregnant? Yet I was bored, alone; at that time I still didn't have any friends.

We moved when I was seven into a townhouse on rue Poussin, where we rented the second floor. On the ground floor lived a little hunchbacked man, a lawyer by profession, M. Lewinsky, who regularly gave me candies. I remember the cast-iron grill that closed off the stairs to the second floor, on which I would swing, shoving off from the stairs. The maid at that time was named Jacqueline. She played the accordion on evenings when my parents were out, and one Sunday afternoon took me to the Châtelet theater, where her mother was a cook, to see *Les Cloches de Corneville*. The maid's boyfriend was a "wog" (as we then called them) from North Africa but I wasn't permitted to read newspapers to keep up on things like that. I would listen to "La famille Duraton." I was taken to see the series "Papa, mama, the maid, and me" with Robert Lamoureux on the Champs Élysées.

We still didn't have a telephone line of our own, and calls had to go through the building's owner, Dr. Billot, whose mustache was as yellow as the bottom of the bathtub that we could use with his permission. He lived on the third floor in the company of a none-too-friendly Polish woman, Wanda. We had no refrigerator either, since I remember the long slabs of ice that were brought up, dripping, in a basket. But we had the use of a little garden to which I used to invite my friends for hula-hoop sessions. One day, I secretly had an old dream fulfilled: I traded my dear Trilby books—*Dadou, a Paris kid*, which had moved me so, and *The Silver Skates*, reread so many times—for a box of parlor games that my parents refused to get for me. Thursdays, I would rush to the newsstand to devour *Line, Lisette, Nano and Nanette, Aggie*. Ima took a malicious pleasure in making me sob, claiming that in fact I was not their daughter but the abandoned child of the Count and Countess of Paris. One evening I tried to fly after reading *Peter Pan*; I fell off the mantelpiece. Jacqueline, the accordion-playing maid, introduced me a little later to rock and roll and Elvis Presley.

Opposite us, a bit up the street from the public baths and showers, lived "Clubfoot" and his daughter Christine, who wore such a pretty crown of flowers the day of her private first communion. Like us, they spent the summer on the Basque coast, just a few miles from Sepharad. Sundays, Abba would ceremoniously escort me to have an aperitif, at the Orée du Bois or the Murat. Straws for grenadine were made of straw back then. On our way home, we would stop at Gurmann's pastry shop, then at the Russian Soukanoff's to buy things for the evening meal. Ima always liked her "surrogate son" to have short hair, to have him wear trousers. In 1956, at the moment of the Hungarian Revolution, they seriously thought of adopting a little Hungarian boy.

> My mother went to the market to buy coal,
> She brought me home a little Pole,
> Oh, how handsome and charming is the little lad,
> With his dark little eyes, my own pussycat.[3]

Then it was rue Molitor, the "Diabolo menthe" years. I finally had a room to myself. Abba, for his part, still had to sleep on the sofa in the living room. My room looked out on Villa Molitor, just up from the gardens of a count whose very upper-crust receptions I spied on. A bit further along, the townhouse belonging to Marie-France, and the cellar where I falsified so many report cards, where we had our first surprise parties. On the sidewalk opposite, the even-numbered side, was Irène's building. And opposite the Metro, Élisabeth's apartment. Her father, a burly Alsatian widower, made me think of that popular scary figure, M. le Maudit.

I remember discovering the books *Claudine at School*, *Girls in Uniform*, *The Dialogue of the Carmelites*, the song from the movie *Exodus*, "Song of the Partisans," and "Sag warum." I paid Josette in Gaucho candies from Murat-Délices to make the baby clothes we had to sew for class. Monique never tired of accompanying me back to the door of my building, but when the hour for the program *Hi, Pals* came, I left her in the lurch. I remember the Molitor skating rink and the smell of the Schmidt shop where I had my skates sharpened, the turnabout at la Muette and its crowd of kids hanging around, the drugstore on the Champs Élysées where we would go to look for the addresses of Sunday parties to crash while eating banana splits and, from later, I remember the Scossa on place Victor-Hugo.

Coming out from a showing of *Night and Fog*, I had my first period. Ima, very proud, rushed to trumpet the news to her sisters, her friends: "Sara has become a young woman!" She showed me how to put on sanitary napkins but warned me, "Tomorrow morning, if you can't manage it, don't wake me up. Ask your father." At high school, each of us kept a lookout for the first brassiere of a classmate, a Teen-form, under the horrid grayish blouse with our initials embroidered in red or blue, depending on the week, in the pockets of which lay the dental braces of childhood mixed in among shavings from the pencil sharpener.

It was in front of the newsstand at the Michel-Ange-Molitor Metro station, one morning like all the others on my way to high school, that I read the headline "Eichmann hanged." That evening, Abba seemed relieved.

The Twist Years lasted only long enough for me to repeat a year of high school. All at once and all together, I discovered love, literature,

The Rules of the Game, A Mad Love, All Boys Are Called Patrick, Hitler Who?, philosophy . . . soon the University of Nanterre-la-folie. When Abba thought he understood that I was no longer a virgin, he cried to begin with.

A la una yo nasi,
A las dos me engrandesi,
A las tres tomi amante.

I was born at one o'clock,
By two I had grown up,
At three I took a lover.[4]

I will always remember that beach near Athens where I saw, moving away from me, as if in a black-and-white Fellini dream, my grave and mute parents, together, side by side, united, it would seem, in their distress. I learned that in the East maidenheads could be resewn.

"Is Ima there?" I would ask as soon as I got home from school and Rosario, Amparo, Clementina, or whoever in a pink- or blue-striped smock (depending on the week) had opened the door for me. Ima was often not there. When this was the case, she cultivated an absent presence. Behind a stubbornly closed door, the prostrate woman fixed her disappointed and empty eyes on a window opening onto nothing. I never got used to Ima's disappearances, as sudden as they were frequent. Autumn is a bad season for the depressed. Electric shocks were then a fashionable therapy; no one ever suggested Ima talk her way to a cure. Similarly, ergotherapy was very popular; Ima was quite happy to have learned how to weave baskets. She usually spent three weeks on a sleep cure during which they tried to struggle against her chronic insomnia. I remember, however, a ritual meticulously carried out in the room that we had been sharing for so long, the fetid smell of the barbiturate Supponeryl that even lavender water sprinkled on a handkerchief pressed against your nose did not dissipate. I remember the row of little bottles and drip tubes on the mantelpiece, the herbal tea that Ima had boiled on a little makeshift hot plate even when she was on holiday, long hours of reading in the middle of the night. In order not to disturb me, Ima would put a sheet of newspaper over the light shade, which often caught on fire.

We didn't have permission to visit Ima at the Meudon clinic, nor to telephone her. Her "state" required that she cut all ties. At times, however, when her absence seemed to have gone on forever, Abba relaxed the rules. On Sunday, he would take me to the long wall and would hoist me up on the roof of the Simca. Between the curtain of trees of the huge parkland, from a high window of one of the numerous pavilions, I could make out a lifeless hand that waved in our direction, briefly, only briefly, then the window closed again, quickly, so quickly. My heart seemed clenched when we went into the tunnel that took us back to Paris. I always hated Meudon. When Ima came home again, no noise was to be made behind that door now closed once again. When lithium appeared on the market, we had some cause for hope. You scrupulously submitted to complex dosings. You rediscovered laughter, you took an interest in your family again. But soon your blood count was affected. You had to stop, and the restless moves between one medication and another began again.

Much later, when Abba, exhausted and almost at the end of his tether, capitulated, it was I who drove my mother to her psychiatrist's appointments. I remember Ima's last time in the hospital at La Salpetrière. The famous professor received me, relieved to "finally meet someone reasonable in this family!" Then the diagnosis was uttered, brutally short and to the point: "precocious senility," "senile dementia." You were only 62, you poor dear. Other diagnoses followed: "clinophile"—you appeared, in fact, more secure, calmer, inside the walls of your prisons, sheltered from Jacob's tenderness— "manic-depressive." You lost your ability to walk, then your desire to speak, you became a shape under a sheet. You refused to eat. "You're crazy, crazy like your mother," my own aunt Sultana shouted at me one evening.

What *dibuk* could have possessed Ima when she rushed at me, still a small child, forcing the pepper mill into my mouth when I had broken the mica window of the stove with my toy shovel in my impatience to go out?

What dibuk could have possessed Esther, supine whole Sundays in the walnut sleigh bed on the edges of which I slid to pass the time?

The dibuk of Esther about which I learned when leafing through the bills for stays in the psychiatric hospital: the fact that she wanted to convert—but why had they put her in Sion and not at the Alliance?—that she thought she was a saint. You were born, Ima, on 17 March 1921. The date of the genocide of the Jews living in the empire, planned by Haman the Persian vizier, had been set for the 13th of Adar (beginning of March). *Purim, purim lanou pesah en la mano.*[5] Purim, the most joyous of Jewish holy days, the one when gifts of sweets were made: *mandar plato . . . kon orejas de Aman.* Papu must have read you the *megila* of Esther. Like Queen Esther, by changing your surname, your first name, your nationality, did you hope to hide your appearance, your origin?

The dibuk of Esther whose body, crossed with inflamed stripes, elicited as sole diagnosis from a famous professor of dermatology, "In the Middle Ages they would have burned you as a witch." The Inquisition didn't end until 1834. A century later Hitler took power.

The dibuk of Esther calling the police when she had herself succeeded in pulling the bolts of the entry door with the tips of her terribly arthritic fingers.

The dibuk of my mother that I sensed when I had gone to fetch her so that she could have a walk with her grandson, delightedly starting up, in the middle of the street, with "Allons enfants . . . qu'un sang impur" (from the "Marseillaise"). The year 1447: first regulations concerning *limpieza de sangre*; 1935: the Nuremberg laws.

The dibuk of Esther threatening Jacob with a knife.

The dibuk of Esther that, at the sight of the smoke coming out of the fireplace in the psychiatrist's office during the consultation, mocked the "spirits," interpreting the ambulance sirens as a carillon of bells. People spoke indirectly of a bout of meningitis that you had had as a small child. "Perhaps it's hereditary, runs in the family," your cousin Beky wrote me upon hearing of the progress of your ordeal. When she learned of the departure of her daughter for Ankara, where she was to be married, didn't Beky's paternal grandmother cry out at every moment, "Oh, there is Vintoura! Oh, she's in the tree, can't you see her?" Like you, she didn't want to eat.

The dibuk of Esther—incapable of calling for help?—when Jacob lay half-unconscious in his bathtub for forty-eight hours.

> *Adio, adio kerida,*
> *No kiero la vida,*
> *Me la amargastes tu.*

> Farewell, my love,
> I want no more of life,
> you have made it too bitter for me.[6]

Esterika, Rozika, my dear little Ima, what happened to you? That witch's mask, I couldn't bear it. The terrible images that you inflicted on me. But I have so many others in reserve, my beautiful Ima. When you were so radiant the times my little friends came to get me to go dancing—me who was like Mohammed's mount, *ni pesce ni carne*—that they only had eyes for you, poor dear who danced so little in those old people's hotels, as you said. *Com' è bella, la tua mamma!* But I was cruel then: "*Se la vedessi la matina!* Do you remember me dancing the twist for the first time in Saint-Tropez in the bell-bottomed trousers from Chez Choses? You went with me to the nightclubs, and my dates took care to dance a tango with you first. You liked to flirt with my friends. In Gstaad you showed yourself in your nightgown to one of them. I wore awfully dull underwear compared to yours. You didn't want anyone to make out my stomach, my breasts, in clothes that were too clinging; that you reserved for yourself. Yet you took me to the big fashion houses. I was covered in silk, a very stylish young lady. The dressmaker used to come to the house. The beautician and the masseur as well. In that apartment that we didn't even own, in the midst of that furniture that you had had so much trouble and so much pleasure in buying yourself, that I didn't even know how to keep up for you when the time came . . . little Ima, I feel so bad, I can't find the words. Sometimes you would ask me, "How long will I be able to stay here? Do I have enough money?" My throat would tighten, Ima. For which monstrous crime were you being punished there?

In three days, you'll already be five years old, my little dead Ima. Five years, already, during which I no longer pushed on that always open door, Broca, East Wing, fourth floor. But how can you lie like that, your back to the door, without the least curiosity, without the least fear that someone could threaten you, without trying to escape from your torpor, to break that infinite duration structured by nothing, since you no longer even knew what year, what day, what hour it was, didn't even ask me any more? But why did they continue to offer you calendars?

Five years since you last raved over the little Benoît—Baruch!—that you would have had with your childhood friend Sadi Saban. Five years since you claimed that you had remarried someone other than Jacob.

Five years since I cried at the stop of bus 83 that took me from rue d'Assas to boulevard Arago, five years since I have gone around Broca without taking the decision to face up to the unbearable.

Five years since I heard your nurse, dear M. Perrot, enumerate for me all the catastrophes of which you, his "boarders," were the survivors.

Five years since I unlearned to be the mother of my mother.

Five years since I talked in my head to Abba in order to justify myself, in order to assure him that you were not so badly off "over there," in *Pitchipoï*.

Five years since I became an orphan. Five years since I learned that mothers are mortal. Five years that I have had no past. Five years since I stopped being somebody's child.

Five years since anyone talked to me of you, of you two. *No yores, mi alma.*

Yom Kippur 5760. *Shana tova!* Is that how it's written? This year too I would spend the holidays alone, sit by myself and listen to the Kol Nidre on Radio J, the only one excluded from the community. I had never known what belonging to the community, belonging to any community, saying "us," meant. Alone over the graves of my parents, unless I had once again postponed the meeting. I had never been able to find the resolve to visit my father, nor my mother when she in turn abandoned me. What could be happening inside? At bottom, at the very bottom, grandmother Rébecca, hated by Ima, the one they had let die in the hotel on boulevard Richard-Lenoir. Yet it was beside Abba's office, and he used to visit her morning and evening. Above, Abba. On the first level, Ima. Were they still quarreling? A burial plot good for a hundred years. Not a single little pebble attesting to your memory. And me, where will I go? There's no longer any place for me. Cremated? Not a Jewess.

"You are eternal, you will never die, you will not leave me alone, you can't do that to me," I would say, stamping my feet, a child.

"*Kukla mia, kokona*, you'll have to manage on your own," Abba would assure me, taking me on his warm knees.

Unable to get over the death of my parents, I had to go looking for them, had to appropriate their lives, their lives from before I came into the world. What do you do in front of a grave when you don't know how to pray? You remember. A day didn't go by that I didn't think of them, that I didn't remember some happy day, a song, my mother's melancholy, my father's eyes, voice, his hands, his smile. What was I doing at this grave? How to pray? Which words to chose? Which language? I would tell them how much I missed them, how I couldn't live in their absence, I would say to them the words they had said to me when I was little, when I was a teenager, I would tell them of the time I wasted by not daring to say how close I was to them, and why I had so long pretended indifference and scorn. I would tell them how much their passionate quarrels, their sense of drama that always exhausted me, were now missed.

This Yom Kippur I will go, I will tell them, without fail, unless I am in Jerusalem. *Al anyo ke viene en tyerra de Israel*, next year in Jerusalem, the promise renewed to my cousin Tico who was pressing me, who was no longer so young.

Notes

Foreword

1. See Sylvie Courtine-Denamy, *Three Women in Dark Times: Edith Stein, Hannah Arendt, Simone Weil,* trans. G. M. Goshgarian (Ithaca, N.Y.: Cornell University Press, 2001).

2. The fine book of Haïm Vidal Sephiha, *L'Agonie des judéo-espagnols* (Paris: Entente, 1977), provides the essentials for those who would like an overview of the history of the language and information on contemporary efforts to consolidate it.

3. Hannah Arendt, "Was bleibt? Es bleibt die Muttersprache" (What remains? The mother tongue remains), in *Gespräche mit Hannah Arendt,* ed. Adelbert Reif (Munich: Piper, 1976), pp. 9–34.

4. Eliezer Ben-Yehuda, *Le Rêve traversé* (Paris: Desclée de Brouwer, 1998).

5. Cf. Stéphane Moses, "Langage et sécularisation," in *L'Ange de l'histoire* (Paris: Le Seuil, 1992), chap. 9.

I In the Land of Sepharad

1. "Zakhor!"

1. "La vida es un pasaje," Judeo-Spanish song performed by Angel Carril, *Tresoro sefardita,* Saga, 1992.

2. Isaac Bashevis Singer, "The Man Who Came Back," in *The Spinoza of Market Street* (New York: Farrar, Strauss and Cudahy, 1961).

3. E. Benbassa and A. Rodrigue, *Juifs des Balkans, espaces judéo-ibériques, XIVe–XXe siècles* (Paris: La Découverte, 1993).

4. Translated from Bernard Lazare, *Le Fumier de Job* (Paris: Circé, 1990).

5. *La Vallée des pleurs* (The Valley of Tears), French trans. by Julien Sée (Paris: Centre d'études Don Isaac Abravanel).

2. Cuenca, the Memory of Origins

1. J. P. Martir Rizo, *Historia de la muy noble y leal ciudad de Cuenca* (1629; Barcelona: El Albir, 1979).

2. L. Poliakov, *L'Histoire de l'antisémitisme de Mahomet aux marranes* (Paris: Calmann-Lévy, 1961).

3. Y. Baer, *History of the Jews in Spain* (Philadelphia: Jewish Publication Society of America, 1978).

4. Don Dimaz Perez Ramirez, "La Sinagoga de Cuenca, Iglesia de Santa Maria La Nueva," *Revista Cuenca* 20, nos. 19–20 (1982).

5. Deut. 28.8.

6. M. Escamilla Collin, *Crimes et châtiments dans l'Espagne inquisitoriale*, preface by P. Chaunu (Paris: Berg International, 1992).

7. *Talmud Nida*, 17a.

8. H.-C. Lea, *Histoire de l'Inquisition au Moyen Age: L'Inquisition dans les divers pays de la Chrétienté*, trans. Salomon Reinach (Paris: Jérôme Millon, 1988).

9. Escamilla Collin, *Crimes et châtiments*.

10. J. M. Pérez-Prendes Muñoz-Arraco, "El procedimiento inquisitorial, esquema y significado," in *La Explusión de los Judios de España* (Toledo: El Curso de Cultura hispano-judia y sefardi, 1992).

11. "Registro del Sello," quoted in L. S. Fernandez, *Documentos acerca de la expulsión de los judios* (Valladolid: Consejo Superior de Investigaciones Cientificas, 1964).

12. It was, in fact, rumored that Ferdinand had a Jewish great-grandmother. See E. Capsali, *Chronique de l'expulsion*, ed. Simone Sultan-Bohbot (Paris: Le Cerf, 1994).

13. Ibid.

14. See E. Benbassa and A. Rodrigue, *Juifs des Balkans, espaces judéo-ibériques, XIVe–XXe siècles* (Paris: La Découverte, 1993).

II Into the Lands of the Grand Turk

1. See E. Benbassa and A. Rodrigue, *Juifs des Balkans, espaces judéo-ibériques, XIVe–XXe siècles* (Paris: La Découverte, 1993).

2. A term used to designate Jews present in Greece from about 85 B.C.E., hellenized and living in the Byzantine Empire, the "Second Rome."

3. A. Pulido, *Españoles sin patria y la raza sefardi* (Madrid, 1807; reprint, Grenada: Universidad de Grenada, 1993).

4. E. Benbassa, "Dans les profondeurs de la mer," *Mémoires juives d'Espagne et du Portugal* (Paris: Publisud, 1996).

5. Pulido, *Españoles sin patria*.

6. Ibid., p. 5.

7. Benbassa and Rodrigue, *Juifs des Balkans*.

1. *Varna: "Cuenca Brothers"*

1. A mythical character to whom great audacity was attributed.

2. *Historia de la Chevra Chessed ve-Emet de Rischuk desde su fondacion 1864 fin la celebracion de su jubileo 1914* (Ruse, 1914).

3. Book of Tobit, 6.12.

4. Lev. 18.6.

5. "Se paseava Silvana," *Chansons judéo-espagnoles*, performed by Hélène Engel, Autour du Monde.

6. *Shulhan Arukh*, "Even ha-Ezer," 15.

2. Salonika

1. S. Usque, quoted in E. Benbassa and A. Rodrigue, *Juifs des Balkans, espaces judéo-ibériques, XIVe–XXe siècles* (Paris: La Découverte, 1993).

2. L. Valensi and N. Wachtel, eds., *Mémoires juives* (Paris: Gallimard, 1986).

3. "La Serena," *Kantes djudeos espanyoles*, performed by Fortuna, La Prima Vez, 1993.

4. F. Schulmann, comp., *L'Enfance ailleurs: Mémoires juives* (Paris: Clancier Guénaud, 1980).

5. *Bulletin* (Paris: Alliance Israélite Universelle, 1899).

6. Vidas Largas, *Chants judéo-espagnols: De Tétouan à Oran*, performed by Henriette Hazan.

7. Valensi and Wachtel, *Mémoires juives*.

8. Isaac Jack Levy, trans., *And the World Stood Silent: Sephardic Poetry of the Holocaust* (Urbana: University of Illinois Press, 1989), pp. 168–69.

3. Constantinople

1. "Las tres ermanikas," Judeo-Spanish song, performed by Joaquin Diaz, *Todas las voces de Sefarad*, Saga, 1988.

2. Num. 9.15.

3. A. Pulido, *Españoles sin patria y la raza sefardi* (Madrid, 1807; reprint, Grenada: Universidad de Grenada, 1993).

4. First stanza of the poem "Der Erlkönig" by Goethe.

5. Lullaby by Brahms.

6. M. Mila y Fontanals, *De la poesía heróico-popular castellano* (1896; reprint, Barcelona: Consejo Superior de Investigaciones Científicas, 1959).

7. Elias Canetti, *The Tongue Set Free: Remembrance of a European Childhood* (New York: Seabury Press, 1979).

8. Letter to the Ministry of Foreign Affairs, 22 March 1922, quoted in J. Ouahnon, "La politique de l'Espagne à l'égard des Juifs de 1925 à 1945," *Les Nouveaux Cahiers* 72.

III Between East and West

1. The Cuenca Michpaha

1. Vicky Tamir, *Bulgaria and Her Jews: The History of a Dubious Symbiosis* (New York: Sepher Hamon Press for Yeshiva University Press, 1979).

2. Ibid.

3. *Le Sauvetage des Juifs en Bulgarie, 1941–1944* (Sofia: Editions Septemviri, 1977).

4. E. Benbassa, *Une vie judéo-espagnole à l'Est: Gabriel Arié* (Paris: Le Cerf, 1992).

5. Ibid.

6. Jean Racine, *Esther*, act 1, scene 2.

2. The Gabay Michpaha

1. "Piyyut del kavritiko," from "Cantos judeo-españoles de Marruecos, recogidos en la Communidad Israelita de Madrid, en homenaje a Maimonides 850 aniversario," in *Todas las voces de Sefarad* (Saga, 1988).

2. Serge Klarsfeld, *L'Étoile des Juifs: Témoignages et documents* (Paris: L'Archipel, n.d.).

3. Ibid.

4. Ibid.

5. A. Pulido, *Españoles sin patria y la raza sefardi* (Madrid, 1807; reprint, Grenada: Universidad de Grenada, 1993).

6. Bielinky, quoted in Klarsfeld, *L'Étoile des Juifs.*

IV Drancy

1. The Return

1. J. Danville and S. Wichene, *Drancy la Juive ou la Seconde Inquisition* (Paris: A. Breger Frères, 1945).

2. R. Poznanski, *Être juif en France pendant la Seconde Guerre mondiale* (Paris: Hachette, 1994).

3. Ibid.

4. Danville and Wichene, *Drancy la Juive.*

5. Ibid.

6. E. Benbassa, *Histoire des Juifs de France* (Paris: Seuil, 1997).

7. M. Rajsfus, *Drancy, un camp de concentration très ordinaire (1941–1944)* (Paris: Manya, 1991).

8. Poznanski, *Être juif en France.*

9. E. Benbassa, *Juifs des Balkans: espaces judéo-ibériques, XIVe–XXe siècles* (Paris: La Découverte, 1993).

10. Poznanski, *Être juif en France.*

2. From the Partisans to the Camps of Upper Silesia

1. P. F. Rousseau, *Intact aux yeux du monde* (Paris: Hachette, 1987), reissued under the name of Robert Frances and the title *Un déporté brise son silence* (Paris: L'Harmattan, 1998).

2. Ibid., p. 140.

3. "In this world we suffer for being Jews. Will we suffer in the next one for not having been Jews?" E. Saporta y Beja, *En torno de la Torre Blanka* (Madrid: Vidas Largas, 1979; French translation, Paris, 1982).

4. M. Rajsfus, *Drancy*.

5. Poznanski, *Être juif en France*.

6. Danville and Wichene, *Drancy la Juive*.

7. Ibid.

8. CDJC, no. XXXVIII-1, quoted in Rajsfus, *Drancy*.

9. R. Poznanski, *Être juif en France pendant la Seconde Guerre mondiale* (Paris: Hachette, 1994).

10. Ibid.

11. Ibid.

12. CDJC, no. DLXII (129) and (130), quoted in Rajsfus, *Drancy*.

13. CDJC archives.

14. Rousseau, *Intact aux yeux du monde*.

15. CDJC, no. DLXII (131), quoted in Rajsfus, *Drancy*.

16. Paul Dumont, "La condition juive en Turquie à la fin du XIXe siècle," *Les Nouveaux Cahiers* 57.

17. Alliance Israélite Universelle, letter no. 441/2, 14 January 1912.

18. Alliance Israélite Universelle, letter no. 466/2, Brusa.

19. R. Frances, "Non, tu ne seras plus là," *Los Muestros* 13 (December 1993).

3. Bayonne and Its Jews

1. H. Léon, *Histoire des Juifs de Bayonne* (Paris, 1893; reprint, Marseilles: Lafitte Reprints, 1976).

2. A. Zinc, "Les Juifs de Saint-Esprit-lès-Bayonne et le prêt à la grosse aventure," *Archives juives, revue d'histoire des Juifs de France* 29, no. 2 (1996).

3. G. Nahon, "Bayonne dans la Diaspora," *Métropoles et périphéries sépharades d'Occident* (Paris: Le Cerf, 1993).

4. *Chansons judéo-espagnoles*, performed by Hélène Engel, Autour du Monde.

5. Quoted in A. Lévi, *Les Vestiges de l'espagnol et du portugais chez les Israélites de Bayonne* (Bayonne: Imprimerie "du Courrier," 1936).

6. It was he who, in a letter of 6 July 1942, wrote to the commissariat for Jewish affairs: "It seems particularly dangerous to me to let the Jewish population know that it may expect a vast, new deportation program," CDJC, no. XXVIII-31a, quoted in Rajsfus, *Drancy*.

7. R. Terrisse, *Bordeaux, 1940–1944* (Paris: Librairie académique Perrin, 1993).

8. Kommando der Sicherheitspolizei und des Sicherheitsdienstes. Gérard Boulanger, *Maurice Papon, un technocrate français dans la collaboration* (Paris: Seuil, 1994).

9. B. Lambert, *Dossiers d'accusation: Bousquet, Papon, Touvier: Inculpés de crimes contre l'humanité* (Éditions de la Fédération nationale des Déportés et internés résistants et patriotes).

10. Terrisse, *Bordeaux.*

11. "C.F.L.N.—Commissariat à l'Intérieur. Service Courrier. Documentation et Diffusion. Dossier B. 29352. Informations diverses. Date: Réception 4-4-44. Diffusion 4-7-44. No. 5087. Informations diverses. Bordeaux" (CDJC, no. CCXIV, 72).

12. Edited and published by Beata and Serge Klarsfeld, BP 137-16, 75763 Paris.

13. Terrisse, *Bordeaux.*

14. *Une Française juive est revenue (Auschwitz, Belsen, Raghun)* (Paris: Éditions du Livre Français, 1945).

15. CDJC archives.

16. Ibid.

V In French Territorial Waters

1. A Wedding Night at the Péra Palas

1. "Las suegras de agora," Judeo-Spanish songs of the eastern Mediterranean, performed by Bienvenida "Berta" Aguado and Loretta "Dora" Gerassi, Maison des Cultures du monde (not released).

2. In the House of Jacob

1. E. Saporta y Beja, *En torno de la Torre Blanca* (Madrid: Vidas Largas, 1979; French translation, Paris, 1982).

2. "Mi Suegra," eastern version, *Chansons judéo-espagnoles*, performed by Hélène Engel, Autour du Monde.

3. "Die Mame is gegangen," *Folklore yiddish*, song performed by Talila and the Kol Aviv Ott Azoi troupe, Arion, 1977.

4. "A la una yo nasi," *Kantes djudeos espanyoles*, performed by Fortuna, La Prima Vez.

5. A little tune that is sung on the eve of Purim to celebrate the arrival of springtime and announce the coming of the Passover holiday.

6. "Adio kerida," *Chansons judéo-espagnoles*, performed by Hélène Engel, Autour du Monde.

Glossary

As concerns the spelling of Judeo-Spanish, I have followed the following works:

Attias, Jean-Christophe, and Esther Benbassa. *Dictionnaire de civilisation juive*. Paris: Larousse-Bordas, 1997.
Nehama, Joseph. *Dictionnaire du judéo-espagnol*. Madrid: Consejo Superior de Investigaciones Científicas, 1977.
Perahya, Klara, and Élie Perahya. *Dictionnaire français-judéo-espagnol*. Paris: Langues Mondes, L'Asiathèque, 1998.

Other words in the text and head words in the glossary are generally given in the form in which they were best known to the Sephardic community, especially to the majority who also spoke French; they may differ slightly from transliterations of Hebrew, Aramaic, Arabic, etc. with which readers of English are most familiar.

abba: papa (Hebrew).
abjuratio de levi: mild abjuration (Church Latin).
abjuratio de vehementi: violent abjuration (Church Latin).
Abtransport: evacuation transport order (German).
abudaraho: salted mullet roe (Judeo-Spanish).
Adar: month of the Hebrew calendar, corresponding roughly to the month of March.
Adonai Elohenou: the Eternal, our God (Hebrew).
akeret habayit: the mistress of the house (Hebrew).
al anyo ke viene en tyerra de Israel: the equivalent of: next year in Jerusalem (Judeo-Spanish).
alboraycos: pejorative term for new converts (Spanish).
alevantamos el göç: we go into exile (Judeo-Spanish, with the last word Turkish).
al ijo bohor: to the eldest son (Judeo-Spanish).
aljama: from Hebrew *qahal* 'community'.
aman, aman, aman! mercy, mercy, mercy! (Arabic, lit. 'pardon').
am ehad, safa ahat: one people, one language (Hebrew).
anyos de vida ke le kontes! long may she live! (Judeo-Spanish).
apyo: celery (Spanish).
la araba de la tchika: the little girl's car (Judeo-Spanish).

asi bivas tu! swear by your life! (Judeo-Spanish).

audiencia de la carcel: prison hearing (Spanish).

audiencia publica o continua: public hearing (Spanish).

Ausweis: pass (German).

auto-da-fé: solemn proclamation of a judgment by the Inquisition (Portuguese).

avia sekolos ke la Espanya era su patria: Spain had been their homeland for centuries (Judeo-Spanish).

avvocato: lawyer (Italian).

ay de mana! Maneate, pateba: Come on, Mama! Move, fatty! (Judeo-Spanish).

ay de mi! poor me! (Judeo-Spanish).

ay, madre mia kerida! oh, dear mother! (Judeo-Spanish).

ayin ara: evil eye (Hebrew); see also *ojo*.

baal teshuva: one who leaves the state of sin and returns to the faith (Hebrew).

bagnini: beach attendants (Italian).

banamelololo: nonsense, malarkey (Turkish).

bar mitzvah: ceremony celebrating a boy reaching religious majority at age thirteen (Aramaic-Hebrew, lit. 'son of the commandment').

bat mitzvah: ceremony at the end of which girls reach the age of religious majority at twelve (Aramaic-Hebrew, lit. 'daughter of the commandment').

benadam: very distinguished (Judeo-Spanish, from Hebrew 'son of man,' whence 'truly a man, a man of means').

benditcho, benditcha: blessed. *Benditchas las manos ke tal fizyeron!* Blessed be the hands that did that! *Benditcho seas, Dyo ke no me fizites mujer!* Blessed be Thou, Lord, who didn't make me a woman! (Judeo-Spanish).

bestya kon figura de benadam: animal with a human face (Judeo-Spanish and Hebrew).

beza mezuza i arova pitas: he kisses the *mezuza* while stealing bread (Judeo-Spanish and Hebrew *mezuza*; see the latter).

bivas, kreskas, i grandeskas! best wishes! (Judeo-Spanish, lit. may you live, grow, and become great!).

borekitas: cheese turnovers (Judeo-Spanish).

bravo cherika mia: well done, little dear! (Judeo-Spanish).

brit mila: circumcision ceremony (Hebrew).

buen, buena: good. *Un buen banyo*: a good bath (Spanish); *buenas noches, mama*: good night, mama; *de buena famiya*: from a good family; *hadas, hadas, hadas buenas ke te vengan*: may the good fairies accompany you! *ke lo bueno!* What a sweetie! *oras klaras, oras buenas!* best wishes! *semanadas buenas i claras, shabat shalom*: may your week go well and purely, may the peace of the Sabbath be upon you (Judeo-Spanish).

castillo: castle (Spanish).

charope blanko: lemon marmalade (Judeo-Spanish).

chkenazia: Ashkenazic woman (Judeo-Spanish).

chuetas: pejorative term for Majorcan converts (Judeo-Spanish).

çifut: mocking term for Jews (from Turkish *gihud*).

com' è bella la tua mamma! how beautiful your mother is! (Italian).

como te llamas? what is your name? (Spanish).

conejo: rabbit (Spanish).

contra fama y memoria: to the detriment of reputation and memory (Spanish).

convencido o probado: convicted, proven (Spanish).

conventiculo: secret meeting of crypto-Judaizers (Spanish).

cristianos nuevos: new Christians (Spanish).

cristianos viejos: old Christians (Spanish).

dechala: leave it alone (Judeo-Spanish).

de mi pueblo: of my people (Judeo-Spanish).

dibuk: maleficent spirit that possesses the body of a living person (Yiddish).

djudyo, djudezmo: Castilian Spanish as spoken by exiles from Spain, to which have been added numerous words from countries to which they emigrated (Judeo-Spanish). To be distinguished from *ladino*, which is now used of the loan translation language in which every Hebrew word in a text invariably has a Judeo-Spanish equivalent.

dönme: those who have turned (Turkish).

el Dyo ke te eskape de ojo malo: see *ojo*.

el ke tyene ija: see *ija*.

È morto il nonno: her grandfather has died (Italian).

en riva: see *ija*.

Es djudyo! I de Stambol! He's Jewish! And from Istanbul! (Judeo-Spanish).

Este es de mi pueblo: he is one of us (lit. of my people; Judeo-Spanish).

Eyos tengan bien i mosotros tambien: may they be happy and we too! (Judeo-Spanish).

filas: flaky pastry (Judeo-Spanish).

fuero: municipal charter, hence customary law (Spanish).

garvanso: chickpea (Spanish).

gefährlich: dangerous (German).

gelato al limone: lemon ice-cream (Italian).

gente menuda: the general populace (Spanish).

goy, pl. *goyim*: non-Jew, belonging to the "nations" (Hebrew).

gueso ajeno: outsider, odd man out (Judeo-Spanish).

Gymnasium: secondary school, high school (German).

hadas: see *buen*.

Haggada: a text read on the occasion of the meal celebrating the first two evenings of Passover (Hebrew).

Halakah: rabbinical law founded on the 613 commandments of the Old Testament, which determine all aspects of daily life (Hebrew, lit. 'advance').

halva: honey-based pastry (Turkish).

Hanukah: festival of lights over eight days commemorating the victory of the Maccabees against the occupation and hellenization policy of Antiochus IV Epiphanes (Hebrew).

haroset: mixture of apples, nuts, cinnamon, and wine to commemorate the mortar used by Hebrew slaves to construct the cities of Pharaoh, in which bitter herbs are dipped on the occasion of the Passover seder (Hebrew).

hembra: woman (Spanish); *la hermosa hembra*: the beautiful woman.

hummus: puree of chickpeas (widespread Middle-Eastern term).

hürryet i vatan: liberty and fatherland (Turkish).

ija: daughter, used in a variety of expressions and proverbs.

— *la ija de las vejes*: daughter of one's old age.

— *ija del baba*: your father's girl.

— *el ke tyene ija de kazar i no la kaza, se kaza sola*: he who has a marriageable daughter and does not marry her risks her marrying on her own.

— *ya basta, ija de un mamzer*: that's enough, bastard daughter; *mamzer* 'bastard' (Hebrew), with a hint of cunning.

— *tyene ijas, tyene ansyas*: he who has daughters has worries.

— *tres ijas i una madre, mala vida por su padre*: three daughters and their mother, a bad life for the father.

— *en riva de kyen kuzgo? En riva de la ija de el Rey de Fransa. Eya tenga tus ansyas, i tu sus ganansyas.* For whom am I sewing clothes? For the daughter of the king of France; may she take on your worries and you her advantages.

ijo: son.

— *ijo mio a la eskola tu te iras, i el tudesko te ambezaras*: my son, you will go to school and you will learn German.

— *ijo regalado*: only son.

ima: mama (Hebrew).

imam baïldi: eggplant dish, so named because, they say, the imam enjoyed it so much that he fainted (Turkish).

judería: Jewish quarter of a town or city (Spanish).

kaddish: prayer for the dead (Hebrew, 'sanctification').

kak vy pozhivaete, babushka? How are you, grandmother? (Russian).

kaminos de letche i myel! may your path be filled with milk and honey! (Judeo-Spanish).

karet: divine punishment (Hebrew).

kasher: belonging to *kashrout*, the collection of religious dietary prescriptions, which in particular distinguishes between clean and unclean animals (Hebrew).

kaymak: very thick cream, with a rice base (Turkish).

kefte: small meatballs (Turkish).

ke haber, kerida?: how are you, dear? (Judeo-Spanish).

kehila, pl. *kehilot*: community (Hebrew).

ke lo bueno! see *buen*.

ketuba: marriage contract (Hebrew).

kipa: a skullcap with which devout Jews cover their head (Hebrew).

Kol-Nidre: 'all commitments', the first office on the eve of Yom Kippur, which permits the faithful to free themselves of all vows, obligations, oaths, promises, and commitments of a religious nature that have been contracted during the previous year, made involuntarily or under coercion, as in the case of the *marranos* (Aramaic).

kon eskarinyo: with nostalgia (Judeo-Spanish).

kon salud i kon vida! may you live in good health! (Judeo-Spanish).

la kriatura . . . dos grandes ojos: see *ojo*.

kukla mia, kokona: my little doll, my little dear (Judeo-Spanish).

kurabiyes: pastries, also called gazelle's horns (Turkish).

kyen mal te kere? kyen mal mos kera? who could wish you, us, ill? (Judeo-Spanish).

kyen tyene mujer ermoza, ke la tenga byen guardada: he who has a beautiful wife, let him keep her well watched (Judeo-Spanish).

kyeres un bonbon, hanum, hanumika? do you want a candy, my little dear? (Judeo-Spanish; *hanum*, Turkish).

laban: very thick yogurt that is cut with a knife (Turkish).

le bezo las manos, senyor padre: I kiss you hands, Father (Judeo-Spanish).

Lejli: Pole (Turkish).

liebre: hare (Spanish)

limpio: pure; *limpieza de sangre*: pureness of blood (Spanish).

lindo: beautiful (Spanish).

magen David: the star of David (Hebrew).

malebis: small cream pastries (Judeo-Spanish).

malos cristianos: bad Christians (Spanish).

malsin: informer (Spanish).

mamu: grandmother (from Greek).

mandar plato . . . kon orejas de Aman: offer a pastry in the shape of ears recalling those of Haman (Judeo-Spanish); on the latter, see *megila*.

mangal: charcoal stove (Turkish).

ma nishtanah: how does (this night) differ (from others)? Question traditionally posed by the youngest child of the family at Passover (Hebrew); see *Haggada*.

manzanikas koloradas, las ke vyenen de Stambol: red apples, those that come from Istanbul (Judeo-Spanish).

maravedi: coin struck in Spain that remained in circulation until 1848 (Spanish).

maşallah: God be praised (Turkish, from Arabic); *maşallah, estos i muntcho*: bravo, I wish you many other good things.

matanza: massacre (Spanish).

mazal tov! good luck! (Hebrew).

megila: parchment scroll, in particular that of Esther, read on the feast of Purim, which commemorates Esther and Mordecai saving the Jews whose extermination had been proposed by Haman, the vizier of Assuerus (Hebrew).

meldado: prayer vigil on the anniversary of a death (Judeo-Spanish).

me llamo: my name is (Spanish).

merenda: tea, light afternoon meal (Spanish).

meza franka: open house, lit. free table (Judeo-Spanish).

mezuza: parchment scroll attached to the right doorpost of Jewish houses containing verses from Deuteronomy (Hebrew).

michpaha: family (Hebrew *mishpochah*).

mikve: ritual bath (Hebrew).

minyan: quorum of ten male Jews who have celebrated their *bar mitzvah*, required to recite *kaddish* (Hebrew).

mi padre me kazava i yo no lo savia: my father married me off without my knowing it (Judeo-Spanish).

mitzvah, pl. *mitzvot*: religious obligation ordered by the Torah; in the current language, a good action (Hebrew).

modrisko: a kiss like a bite (Judeo-Spanish).

moshav: Palestinian village farm.

mshtebnia, shtebnet: adopted.

nasido al kanton: born to one side, abandoned (Judeo-Spanish).

ninya: little girl; *la ninya en la facha, la achugar en la kacha*: start a girl's trousseau when she is still in diapers (Judeo-Spanish).

ni pesce ni carne: neither fish nor meat (Italian); cf. English neither fish nor fowl.

nono, nona: grandfather, grandmother (from Italian).

no te merekyes, hanum: don't worry, my dear (Judeo-Spanish).

no yores, mi alma: don't cry, my soul (Judeo-Spanish).

la nuera: see *suegra*.

ojo: eye (Spanish); literally and figuratively in various Judeo-Spanish expressions:

— *el Dyo ke te eskape de ojo malo i de ayin ara!* may God protect you from the evil eye!

— *ojo malo, avla mala, ayin ara ke no mos toke!* may the evil eye, evil words, and envious looks not affect us!

— *la kriatura . . . dos grandes ojos pretos komo azeytunes de Volo*: the child . . . two huge eyes as black as Volos olives.

— *tus ojos no veyan mal!* may your eyes see no evil!

— *o ke lo vide, o ke no lo vide / siera amalgado kon el polvo della tyerra*: whether it is seen or not, it is mixed into the dust of the earth (Judeo-Spanish).

oras klaras: see *buen*.

pan senzeno: unleavened bread (Judeo-Spanish).

papu: grandfather (from Greek).

las paras: money (Judeo-Spanish).

parashah: each of the fifty-two pericopes or weekly lessons from the first five books of the Bible (Hebrew).

pastelikos: little pastries (Judeo-Spanish).

Pesah: Passover, celebrated in the spring, in the month of Nisan, commemorating the end of the Israelites' slavery in Egypt (Hebrew).

peshkado liso: fish without scales (Judeo-Spanish).

primo, prima: cousin (Spanish).

quemadero: stake at which people were burned (Spanish).

raza: race (Spanish).

reconciliación, reconciliados: reconciliation, those reconciled (Spanish).

Reconquista: reconquest of the Iberian peninsula from the Muslims by the Christian kings, begun in the eighth century and completed with the capture of Grenada in 1492 (Spanish).

relajación: the act of delivering those condemned by the Inquisition to the secular arm (Spanish).

restecada: refugee (female) (Judeo-Spanish)

Rosh Hashanah: Jewish New Year, celebrated on the first and second of the month of Tishri, generally between September and October (Hebrew).

sadik, tsadik: righteous (Hebrew).

salveconducto: safe conduct (Spanish).

sanbenito: lit. holy sack (Spanish). The origin of this practice of dressing in brown sackcloth with yellow crosses, which penitents had to wear at the entry to the church or on the steps to the altar for one or two years, goes back to the Old Testament, Achab having been condemned to dress in this fashion after having acquired Nabot's vineyard improperly (1 Kings 1.21).

seder: Passover meal eaten in a very precise sequence (Hebrew).

sefarad tahor: pure Sephardic (*tahor*, Hebrew).

se la vedessi la matina! if you saw her in the morning! (Italian).

semanadas buenas, see *buen*.

señal real: royal seal (Spanish).

sentencia de prueba: juridical proof (Spanish).

shabat: holy day, Friday evening until Saturday evening (Hebrew).

shana tova: Happy New Year (Hebrew).

Shema Israël: Hear! O Israel, Deuteronomy 6.4 (Hebrew).

shiduch: matchmaker (Hebrew).

shofar: ram's horn blown particularly on Rosh Hashanah and to mark the end of the Yom Kippur fast (Hebrew).

simha: joy (Hebrew).

siniza i fumo: ash and smoke (Judeo-Spanish).

sinoga: synagogue (Old Spanish).

son de los muestros: they are of our people (Judeo-Spanish).

sos de la grande famiya? are you part of the large family? (Judeo-Spanish).

sospechosos en la fé: suspect in matters of faith (Spanish).

sposika: little wife (Judeo-Spanish).

stubawas: persons in charge of barracks, here in concentration camps (German).

suegra: mother-in-law (Judeo-Spanish); *la nuera traye achugar de oro i de marfil, la suegra tyene syempre ke dizir*: the daughter-in-law brings a trousseau of gold and ivory but the mother-in-law still makes pointed remarks.

suspectus violenter: violently suspect (Church Latin).

Talmud Torah: community schools where the text of the law is studied (Hebrew).

tchay: tea (Turkish).

tevila: the act of immersion to become Jewish again (Hebrew).

Tish ah b'Ab: ninth day of the month of Av (July-August) which commemorates the destruction of the first temple (586 B.C.E.) and second temple (70 B.C.E.) (Hebrew)

tocino: bacon (Spanish).

Torah: the doctrine of the five books of the law, the Pentateuch (Hebrew).

tornadizos: volatile persons, susceptible to change (Spanish).

tres ijas: see *ija*.

trontcho: core, heart (Judeo-Spanish).

Tsahal: acronym of Tseva Hagana le-Yisrael, the Israeli army (Hebrew).

tsio, tsia: uncle, aunt (from Italian *zio*).

tu boka koma myel: (words from) your mouth (are as sweet) as honey (Judeo-Spanish).

Tudeskos: Germans, Ashkenazic Jews.

tus ojos: see *ojo*.

tyene ijas: see *ija*.

uevos jaminados: pickled eggs (Judeo-Spanish).

ya vino el ninyo! En bien sea venido! A son is born to us, let him be welcome! (Judeo-Spanish).

yalis: wooden palace or manors, typically on the Bosphorus (Turkish).

yangin var!: Fire! (Turkish).

yo te bendigo . . . amen: I bless you, amen (Judeo-Spanish).

Yom Kippur: day of the great pardon, the tenth day of Tishri (September–October), when the observant fast as a sign of repentance (Hebrew).

zakhor: remember (Hebrew, masculine imperative); to his daughter Abba could have said *zekhri*, but he was simplifying.

zito! viva! (Turkish).

zloty: unit of Polish currency.

References

Benbassa, Esther. *Un grand rabbin sépharade en politique, 1892–1923*. Paris: Presses du CNRS, 1990.

———. *Une diaspora sépharade en transition. Istanbul XIXe–XXe siècle*. Paris: Cerf, 1993.

Boulanger, Gérard. *Maurice Papon, un technocrate français dans la collaboration*. Paris: Seuil, 1994.

Cirac Estopanan, Sebastian. *Registro de los documentos del Santo Oficio de Cuenca y de Siguenza*, vol. 1, *Registro General de los Processos de Delitos y de los Expedientes de Limpieza*. Cuenca and Barcelona, 1965.

Collective. *Dossier Les Juifs de France*. Desclée de Brouwer, 1995.

Collective. *Les Juifs d'Espagne, histoire d'une diaspora, 1492–1992*. Paris: Liana Lévi, 1992.

Encyclopedia Judaïca.

Encyclopedia Judaïca Castillana.

Eymerich, Nicolau. *Le Manuel des Inquisiteurs, avec les commentaires de Francisco Pena*. Louis Sala Molins. Paris: Mouton, 1973.

Garcia-Arenal, Mercedes. *Inquisición y moriscos, los processos del tribunal de Cuenca*. Siglo XXI Editores, 1978–1983.

Gœtschel, R. *1492, l'expulsion des Juifs d'Espagne*. [Paris:] Maisonneuve et Larose, 1996.

Graetz, Heinrich. *Histoire des Juifs*, vol. 4, *De l'époque du gaon Saadia (920) à l'époque de la Réforme (1500)*. Trans. Moïse Bloch. Paris, 1893.

Kedourie, Élie. *Le Monde juif: Histoire et civilisation du peuple juif*. London: Fonds Mercator, Thames and Hudson, 1979.

Kriegel, Maurice. "La prise d'une décision, l'expulsion des Juifs d'Espagne en 1492." *La Revue historique* 260, pt. 1, no. 527 (July–September 1978).

———. *Les Juifs à la fin du Moyen Age dans l'Europe méditerranéenne*. Hachette, 1979.

Lacave, José Luis. "L'Espagne à la découverte du séfardisme." *Les Nouveaux Cahiers* 62 (1980): 9–44.

Lea, H. C. *Histoire de l'Inquisition au Moyen Age*, 3 vols. Trans. Salomon Reinach. Jérôme Millon, 1988.

Leroy, Béatrice. *Les Juifs dans l'Espagne chrétienne avant 1492*. Paris: Albin Michel, 1993.

Lévi, Albert. *Les Vestiges de l'espagnol et du portugais chez les Israélites de Bayonne: Le Cimetière israélite de Labastide-Clairance*. Bayonne: Imprimerie du Courrier, 1936.

López Mateo. *Memorias historicas de Cuenca y sú obispado.* Ed. Angel Gonzalez Palencia. Madrid, 1949.

López Martínez, Nicolas. *Los Judaizantes Castellanos y la Inquisición en tiempo de Isabel la Catolica.* Burgos, 1954.

Mechoulan, Henry. *Le Sang de l'autre ou l'Honneur de Dieu (Indiens, Juifs et morisques au Siècle d'or).* Fayard, 1979.

Mitre Fernández, Emilio. *Los Judios de Castilla en tiempo de Enrique III: El Pogrom de 1391.* Estudios de Historia Medieval. University of Valladolid, 1994.

Morin, Edgar. *Vidal et les siens.* Paris: Le Seuil, 1989.

Moulinas, René. *Les Juifs du Pape: Avignon et le Comtat Venaissin.* Paris: Albin Michel, 1992.

Muñoz y Soliva, Trifon. *Historia de la muy Noble y Leal ciudad de Cuenca y del territorio de su provincia y obispado desde los tiempos primitivos hasta la edad presente.* Cuenca, 1866.

Ouahnon, Josette. "La politique de l'Espagne à l'égard des Juifs de 1925 à 1945." *Les Nouveaux Cahiers* 62 (1980): 9–44.

Parondo, C. C., "Un judio castellano frente a la Inquisición." *Cuadernos de Jerusalem,* no. 4 (1997).

———. "Los clerigos judaizantes de Huete." *Annuario de estudios medievales.* Barcelona: Consejo Superior de Investigaciones Cientificas, 1982.

Pérez, Joseph. *Historia de una tragedia: La expulsión de los Judios de España.* Barcelona: Critica, 1993.

Pérez Ramírez, Dimas, and Miguel Jiménez Monteserin. "Cuenca: la sinagoga de Cuenca, iglesia de Santa Maria la Nueva." *Revista Cuenca,* nos. 19, 20 (1982). Editadas por la Excma. Diputación Provincial de Cuenca.

———. "Ruta de la Inquisicion en Cuenca." *La Inquisición española: Nueva vision, nuevos horizontes.* (Ed. Joaquiim Perez Villanueva). Siglo Veintiuno de España Editores, SA.

Roth, Philip. *Patrimony: A True History.* New York: Simon and Schuster, 1991.

Sephia, Haïm Vidal. *L'Agonie des judéo-espagnols.* Paris: Ententes, 1977.

Steinsaltz, Adin. *Hommes et Femmes de la Bible.* Trans. Katy Allouche and Michel Allouche. Paris: Albin Michel, 1990.

Suárez Fernández, Luis. *Les Juifs espagnols au Moyen Age.* Trans. Paris: Gallimard, 1980.

———. *Documentos acerca de la expulsión de los Judios.* Valladolid, 1964.

Torres Fontes, Juan. "Moros, judios y conversos en la regencia de don

Fernando de Antequera." *Cuadernos de Historia de España* 21–22 (1960): 1–97.

Valmaña Vicente, Alfredo. *El fuero de Cuenca.* Introduction, translation, and notes. Editorial Torno Alicante 2. 2d ed. Cuenca, 1978.

Vincent, Bernard. *1492, L'anée admirable.* Aubier, 1991.

Wigoder, G., ed. *Dictionnaire encyclopédique du judaïsme: Esquisse de l'histoire du peuple juif.* Paris: Cerf, 1993.

I n d e x

Note: *pl.* indicates the photographic plates located at the center of the book.

Abenxuxe, Symuel, 16–17
Abjuratio, 14, 20, 22
Abravanel, Isaac, 24–25
Aguilar, Diego de, 54
Ajuelo, David, 121
Ajuelo, Rose, 121
Akşiyote, Angelo, 45
Akşiyote, Moïse and Allegra, 42–47
Akşiyote, Peppo, 45
Albornoz, Sancho, 16
Alfonso VIII, xii, 10–11
Alfonso X, 11
Aljama, 23, 43
Almetabamid ben Abbad, 10
Arditti, Bernhard, 82
Arendt, Hannah, x, xii
Aşkale, *pl.*
Atatürk, Kemal, 43, 53
Auschwitz, xii, 38, 48, 58, 102, 108,
    111, 119–21, 131
Auto-da-fé, 19, 21–23
Avigdor, Albert, 102
Avigdor, Elia, 47, 61–62
Avigdor, Joseph and Klara, 44–47, *pl.*
Avigdor, Marguerite, 47
Avigdor, Mathilde, 47–48
Avigdor, Zelda, 77

Balkan War, 43
Bally, David, 114, 118–21
Bally, Marie, 117–21
Bally, Rachel (Nelly), 38, 55, 57, 114,
    117–21, *pl.*
Baruch, Marcou, 82

Barzilay, Makhlouf, 90, 100, 102, 104
Barzilay, Menahem, 90, 101
Barzilay, Sultana. *See* Gabay, Sultana
Basch, Victor and Hélène, 104, 118
Baum, Judith, 63
Baur, André, 109, 117
Bayezid II, 25
Bechar, Chayim, 81
Benbassat, Albert and Fortunée, 38
Ben Gurion, David, 83
Bensasson, Djemille, 55
Bensasson, Samuel and Elda, 58
Ben-Yehuda, Eliezer, xiii
Biarritz, France, 115
Birnbaum, Suzanne, 119–20
Blum, Robert-Félix, 109–10, 119
Boris III, 80–82
Botton, Vida de, 35–37, *pl.*
Brunner, Aloïs, 48, 108–9

Cabeza de Vaca, Juan, 15
Calabre, Nicolas de, 17
Canetti, Elias, xv, 32, 36, 82
Castro, Americo, 16
Cohen, Joseph, 118
Cohen, Klara, 44–47, *pl.*
Cohen, Lea, 47
Conversos, 13–15
Covo, Avraham Yitschak, 36
Covo, Rika, 36–40, 132, *pl.*
Crémieux, Benjamin, 100
Cuenca, David, 35–40, 55, *pl.*
Cuenca, Diego de, 20
Cuenca, Élise. *See* Salti, Elise

Cuenca, Flora, 38–40, 51, 55–56, *pl.*
Cuenca, Hélène, 104, 118
Cuenca, Isaac, 47–49, 109
Cuenca, Isabel de, 24–25, 29–33
Cuenca, Jacky, 38, 57, *pl.*
Cuenca, Joan de, 19–25, 29–33
Cuenca, Joseph, 35–40, 55, *pl.*
Cuenca, Juan, 15–19
Cuenca, Marguerite, 47–48
Cuenca, Meier, 35–40, 55, 57, 78, *pl.*
Cuenca, Michele, 105
Cuenca, Nelly, 131–32
Cuenca, Peppo, 38–41
Cuenca, Rébecca, 37, 50–51, 56,
    128–29, 136–37
Cuenca, Régine, 4, 50–51, 56–59,
    75–78, *pl.*
Cuenca, Rita, 51–52
Cuenca, Salomon, 5, 35–40, 50–51,
    75, 80
Cuenca, Sara, 134
Cuenca, Yako, 35–37, *pl.*
Cuenca (city), 9–25
    ancient names for, 10
    Inquisition in, 14–25
    pogroms in, 12–13, 15, 23
    synagogue of, 15–16
Cuenca-Denamy, Esther (Rozika),
    xi, 3–5, 58–59, 89, 92–94,
    102–4, 125–45, *pl.*
Cuenca-Denamy, Jacob, 3–7, 32, 35,
    45, 52–59, 126–46
Cuenca *michpaha*, 72–84

De Gaulle, Charles, 47
Dowries, 75–76, 78, 126, 128
Drancy, xv, 97–102, 108–10, 117–20
Duchont, Maurice, 118

Eastern Jewish Teacher Training
    College (ENIO), 6, 66

Eichmann, Adolf, 110, 140
Enrique II, 12–13
Esperanza Society, 55
Evil eye, 32, 60

Fernandès, Catherine de, 115
Fernando III, 11
Fernando V, 16, 23–25
Florez, Francisco, 14
Fonseca-Chacon, David de, 115–16
Frances, Allegra, 106–7, 111–13
Frances, Bohor, 38, 55, 106, 128
Frances, Isaac, 111–12
Frances, Rita, 104–5, 128
Frances, Robert, 106–13
Frances, Sarina, 36, 38, 55, 106
Frances, Victor, 55, 80, 104–5
Frances, Vivette, 106, 110, 113
Franco, Francisco, 67
Franc-Tireurs et Partisans (FTP),
    106–7, 113
Freemasonry, 77–78, 94, 102, 131
Fresne Prison, 107–8

Gabay, Eléonore, 61–69
Gabay, Judith, 63
Gabay, Klara, 89, 94–95, *pl.*
Gabay, Luna, 89, 91, 132, *pl.*
Gabay, Marco, 5–9, 59–69, 89–94,
    pl.
Gabay, Rozika. *See* Cuenca-
    Denamy, Rozika
Gabay, Sultana, 89–91, 94–95,
    99–102, 104, *pl.*
Gabay, Vittali, 63–66, 69, 88–89,
    102, *pl.*
Gabay, Yehezhiel, 59
Gabay *michpaha*, 86–95
Garcia, Leonor, 20
Gomez de Albornoz, Teresa, 13
Gonsalvo de Cuenca, Martin, 17–18

Gonzalez, Juana, 20
Gordon, Yehuda Leib, 30
Gumiel, Barolomé, 14

Hacohen, Joseph, 8, 13
Haddad, Gérard, xiii
Halevi, Salomon, 13
Halevi, Samuel, 12
Halfon, Fortunée, 114, 117–21
Halfon, Isaac, 114, 118–20
Halfon, Maurice, 114, 119
Hebrew, xiii–xiv, 15–17, 30, 53, 61,
  82–83, 116
Henri IV, 115
Herraiz, Isabel, 22
Houlon, Albert, 75–77
Houlon, Régine. *See* Cuenca,
  Régine
Houlon, Rita, 75–76
Huecar River, 10

Incest, 38–39
Innocent VIII, 18
Inquisition, xii, xvi, 14–25, 30, 54, 143
Isaac ibn Zadok, 11
Isabella of Castile, 14–15, 16, 23–25
Ismail beni Dilnun, 10

Jaulus, Paul, 137
Juan II, 13
Judeo-Spanish, x–xvi, 30–32, 53, 55,
  79, 116

Kaddish, 47, 134
Kafka, Franz, xiii
Kaufman, Chaïm Israel, 104
Kaufman, Dora Finkelstein, 104
Kaych, Suzanne, 92
Ketuba, 131
Kraus, Karl, 55
Kun, Béla, 55

Ladino, x, xvi
Lambert, R., 117
Langberg, Emmanuel, 119
Laval, Pierre, 100–102, 109
Lazare, Bernard, 7–8, 25, 30
Lesbians, 10
Levi, Buko, 81
Levi, Fiko, 82
Louis XIV, 115

Maimonides, 59
Malsines, 16
Manual, Albert, 109
Marranism, 16, 31, 42, 52, 77, 88,
  133–34
Martínez, Ferran, 12
Matanzas. See Pogroms
Mehmed II, 29
Mexico, 46
Michpaha, 31
  Cuenca, 72–84
  Gabay, 86–95
Mitakov, Nikola, 79
Mitsvot, 22
Morin, Edgar, 1, 48
Morin, Vidal, 48
Moriscos, 14
Murcia, 14

Nahmias, Moïse, 50–51, *pl.*
Nahmias, Rébecca. *See* Cuenca,
  Rébecca
Nahmias, Sultana, 37
Nahmias, Victoria, 37, 77
Nahoum, Haïm, 52
Nordau, Max, 30
Nuñez, Francisco, 13

Papon, Maurice, 118–19
Pappo, Haïm, 37, 77, 137
Pappo, Isaac, 77–78

Pappo, Lazare, 37
Pappo, Régine. *See* Cuenca, Régine
Pappo, Salomon, 77–78
Pardo, Berthe, 77–78
Pedro I, 12
Pellepoix, Darquier de, 91
Perera, Moïse Lopez, 53–55
Perets, Avner, 48–49
Perez Ramirez, Dimaz, 14–15
Pesach, 66, 89
Pétain, Philippe, 94, 109
Pitchipoï, 111, 145
Pogroms, 12–13, 15, 23, 111
Policar, Hermine, 78, *pl.*
Policar, Jacques, 37
Policar, Léon, 78, *pl.*
Purim, 143

Quiroga, Gaspar de, 14

Raymond, Henri, 106–7
Reconciliados, 20
Reconquista, 8, 10, 23–25, 42, 115
Rodriguez Mexia, Maria, 13
Romaniot, 29
Romano, Albert, 82
Roth, Philip, xiii, 97
Russo, Jacob, 111
Russo-Turkish War, 79

Sabatier, Maurice, 118
Salonika, 42–49
Salti, Élise, 36, 38, 45, 114
Salti, Marie, 114
Salti, Moïse, 38, 114
Salti, Rose, 114
Sanbenito, 19–20, 22
Sancho IV, 12
Santa Maria, Pablo de, 13
Saporta, Raoul, 131
Sarah, in Bible, 38–39, 133–34

Schmidt, Georges, 119
Senior, Abraham, 24–25
Seville, 8, 13
Sixtus IV, 16
"Sol la Sadika" (song), 46–47
Soncino, Esther, 111
Suárez Fernández, Luis, 24
Sucro River, 10
Suleiman the Magnificent, 42

Tarik ben Zeyak, 10
Toledo, 13, 15
Torquemada, Tomás de, 23–25
Trastamara, Enrique, 12

Unamuno, Miguel de, 30
Union général des Israélites de
     France (UGIF), 103–4, 108,
     117

Vallat, Xavier, 91
Varna, 35–41
Vienna, 4, 37–40, 53–55
Vradjali, Victoria ("Vicky"), 37,
     56–59, 78–80, 79–80, 83–84, *pl.*

Wisliceny, Dieter, 48
Witchcraft, 32, 60, 89, 143–44
Women's International Zionist
     Organization (WIZO),
     132
World Zionist Organization, 52

Yiddish, xiii–xiv
Young Turk movement, 33, 52

Zamora, Council of, 12
Zarfati, Isaac, 29
Zevi, Sabbatai, 33
Zionism, xiii, 52, 55, 82–83,
     132